OF LOVE AND HOPE

AVALANCHE BOOKS

Published in Great Britain by Avalanche Books, England.
2010

Printed by SRP, England

British Library Cataloguing in Publication Data. A catalogue
record for this book is available from the British Library.

ISBN 978 1 874392 68 2

For

Dearest O, with all my love

and for

Mr Zenon Rayter, Dr Chris Price, Angie Nicholson,
Lorna Taylor, Mr Jim Cook and Dr Lee Burton

"I feel very angry with cancer a lot of the time.
It just robs people of their mothers.
It makes me cry a lot"

Florrie Darling

Breast Cancer is the most common cancer in the UK.
1 in 9 women will be diagnosed with the disease.
Nearly 46,000 women are diagnosed with breast cancer every
year and nearly 1,000 women die from breast cancer every
month.

BREAST CANCER CARE

Breast Cancer Care is the UK's leading provider of
information, practical assistance and emotional support for
anyone affected by breast cancer. We deliver services to
women and men who have breast cancer, their family, friends
and carers and health care professionals. Every year we
respond to over two million requests for support and
information about breast cancer or breast health concerns. We
are committed to campaigning for better treatment and
support for people with breast cancer and their families.

BREAKTHROUGH BREAST CANCER

Breakthrough Breast Cancer is a pioneering charity dedicated to the prevention, treatment and ultimate eradication of breast cancer. We believe passionately that this disease can be beaten and are determined to save lives and change futures - through research, campaigning and education - removing the fear of breast cancer for good. Our aim is to bring together the best minds and rally the support of all those who have been - or may one day be - affected by the disease.

More women than ever in the UK are surviving breast cancer, thanks to better awareness, better screening and better treatments.

We are making breakthroughs. But there is much more we need to do to eradicate breast cancer.

100% of all profits raised from the sale of this book will be donated to these two tremendous charities.

I would like to extend my heartfelt thanks and gratitude to all the authors (and their agents and publishers) who have given their work and their support so generously and enthusiastically.

I would also like to thank Short Run Press for sponsoring part of the printing costs of this book.

SHORT RUN PRESS LIMITED

Short Run Press Limited
Litho & Digital Printers and Bookbinders
01392 211909 / www.shortrunpress.co.uk

Proudly sponsoring Breast Cancer charities
www.breakthrough.org.uk
www.breastcancercare.org.uk

Contents

I ALMOST WENT TO BED

I almost went to bed
without remembering
the four white violets
I put in the button-hole
of your green sweater

and how I kissed you then
and you kissed me
shy as though I'd
never been your lover

Leonard Cohen

ST KEVIN AND THE BLACKBIRD

And then there was St Kevin and the blackbird.
The saint is kneeling, arms stretched out, inside
His cell, but the cell is narrow, so

One turned-up palm is out the window, stiff
As a crossbeam, when a blackbird lands
And lays in it and settles down to nest.

Kevin feels the warm eggs, the small breast, the tucked
Neat head and claws and, finding himself linked
Into the network of eternal life,

Is moved to pity: now he must hold his hand
Like a branch out in the sun and rain for weeks
Until the young are hatched and fledged and flown.

*

And since the whole thing's imagined anyhow,
Imagine being Kevin. Which is he?
Self-forgetful or in agony all the time

From the neck on out down through his hurting forearms?
Are his fingers sleeping? Does he still feel his knees?
Or has the shut-eyed blank of underearth

Crept up through him? Is there distance in his head?
Alone and mirrored clear in Love's deep river,
'To labour and not to seek reward,' he prays,

A prayer his body makes entirely
For he has forgotten self, forgotten bird
And on the river-bank forgotten the river's name.

Seamus Heaney

DUST OF SNOW

The way a crow
Shook down on me
The dust of snow
From a hemlock tree
Has given my heart
A change of mood
And saved some part
Of a day I had rued

Robert Frost

THE HEALTH SCARE

I'm living with Uncertainty and Fear.
I need to say their names and make them rhyme.
Two monsters. I can't make them disappear.
I'm living with Uncertainty and Fear.
Though abstract nouns are not a good idea,
And abstract nouns with capitals, a crime,
I'm living with Uncertainty and Fear.
It helps to say their names and make them rhyme.

Wendy Cope

PORTRAIT IN FADING COLOURS

I painted you
Playful in bower shadow
Where whistling jacks grow
Arboured by dusk.
You beckoned me,
Reclining clover veiled like
An uncertain bride,
From the time when we were
Younger and watched
Lumpsuckers skim the millpond.

Chris Tutton

LOVE IS ENOUGH

Love is enough: though the World be a-waning,
And the woods have no voice but the voice of complaining,
    Though the sky be too dark for dim eyes to discover
The gold-cups and daisies fair blooming thereunder,
Though the hills be held shadows, and the sea a dark wonder,
    And this day draw a veil over all deeds pass'd over,
Yet their hands shall not tremble, their feet shall not falter;
The void shall not weary, the fear shall not alter
    These lips and these eyes of the loved and the lover.

William Morris

LATE LOVE

How they strut about, people in love,
How tall they grow, pleased with themselves,
Their hair, glossy, their skin shining.
They don't remember who they have been.

How filmic they are just for this time.
How important they've become - secret, above
The order of things, the dreary mundane.
Every church bell ringing, a fresh sign.

How dull the lot that are not in love.
Their clothes shabby, their skin lustreless;
How clueless they are, hair a mess; how they trudge
Up and down the streets in the rain,

Remembering one kiss in a dark alley,
A touch in a changing room, if lucky, a lovely wait
For the phone to ring, maybe, baby.
The past with its rush of velvet, its secret hush

Already miles away, dimming now, in the late day.

Jackie Kay

TOO HEAVY

Dear Doctor,
I am writing to complain about these words
you have given me, that I carry in my bag
lymphatic, nodal, progressive, metastatic
They must be made of lead. I haul them everywhere.
I've cricked my neck, I'm bent
with the weight of them
palliative, metabolic, recurrent
and when I get them out and put them on the table
they tick like bombs and overpower my own
sweet tasting words
orange, bus, coffee, June
I've been leaving them
crumpled up in pedal bins
where they fester and complain.
diamorphine, biopsy, inflammatory
and then you say
Where are your words Mrs Patient?
What have you done with your words?
Or worse, you give me that dewy look
Poor Mrs Patient has lost all her words, but shush,
don't upset her. I've got spares in the files.
Thank god for files!
so I was wondering,
Dear Doctor, if I could have
a locker
my own locker
with a key.
I could collect them
one at a time,

and lay them on a plate

morphine-based, diagnostically,

with a garnish of
lollipop, monkey, lip

Julia Darling

THE AIR WAS WARM, THE DAY WAS LONG

All afternoon
We gathered each other in
Like harvest, golden.

Fingers, lips, made sense
Of time, its immanence
Slowly unfolding. How

Still we lay. Long shadows
Crept over us, the glass
Of wine, the bread, unbroken.

No gesture, utterance
Or movement to disturb
This moment's pause. It held us

Still as the stone
Within the plum, its secret
Joy, its utter fullness.

And the sun went down on our bed.
The day ended.
However tight we clung, however silent

The night, inside which now,
That moment – boundless,
Flowering anew –

Opens and opens. Sorrow
Belongs to time, passes with time. All joy
Is of this stillness.

Katrina Porteous

We are all in the gutter
but some of us are looking at the stars

Oscar Wilde

PROVISIONS

What should we have taken
with us? We never could decide
on that; or what to wear,
or at what time of
year we should make the journey

So here we are in thin
raincoats and rubber boots

on the disastrous ice, the wind rising

Nothing in our pockets

But a pencil stub, two oranges
Four Toronto streetcar tickets

and an elastic band holding a bundle
of small white filing cards
printed with important facts.

Margaret Atwood

AND DEATH SHALL HAVE NO DOMINION

And death shall have no dominion.
Dead men naked they shall be one
With the man in the wind and the west moon;
When their bones are picked clean and the clean bones gone,
They shall have stars at elbow and foot;
Though they go mad they shall be sane,
Though they sink through the sea they shall rise again;
Though lovers be lost love shall not;
And death shall have no dominion.

And death shall have no dominion.
Under the windings of the sea
They lying long shall not die windily;
Twisting on racks when sinews give way,
Strapped to a wheel, yet they shall not break;
Faith in their hands shall snap in two,
And the unicorn evils run them through;
Split all ends up they shan't crack;
And death shall have no dominion.

And death shall have no dominion.
No more may gulls cry at their ears
Or waves break loud on the seashores;
Where blew a flower may a flower no more
Lift its head to the blows of the rain;
Though they be mad and dead as nails,
Heads of the characters hammer through daisies;
Break in the sun till the sun breaks down,
And death shall have no dominion.

Dylan Thomas

TO A STRANGER

Passing stranger! you do not know
How longingly I look upon you,
You must be he I was seeking,
Or she I was seeking,
(It comes to me as of a dream)

I have somewhere surely
Lived a life of joy with you,
All is recall'd as we flit by each other,
Fluid, affectionate, chaste, matured.

You grew up with me,
Were a boy with me or a girl with me,
I ate with you and slept with you, your body has become
Not yours only nor left my body mine only.

You give me the pleasure of your eyes,
Face, flesh, as we pass,
You take of my beard, breast, hands,
In return,

I am not to speak to you, I am to think of you
When I sit alone or wake at night, alone
I am to wait, I do not doubt I am to meet you again,
I am to see to it that I do not lose you.

Walt Whitman

TRUE LOVE

In the middle of the night, when we get up
after making love, we look at each other in
complete friendship, we know so fully
what the other has been doing. Bound to each other
like mountaineers coming down from a mountain,
bound with the tie of the delivery room,
we wander down the hall to the bathroom, I can
hardly walk, I wobble through the granular
shadowless air, I know where you are
with my eyes closed, we are bound to each other
with huge invisible threads, our sexes
muted, exhausted, crushed, the whole
body a sex - surely this
is the most blessed time of my life,
our children asleep in their beds, each fate
like a vein of abiding mineral
not discovered yet. I sit
on the toilet in the night, you are somewhere in the room,
I open the window and snow has fallen in a
steep drift, against the pane, I
look up, into it,
a wall of cold crystals, silent
and glistening, I quietly call to you
and you come and hold my hand and I say
I cannot see beyond it. I cannot see beyond it.

Sharon Olds

CARRYING MY WIFE

I carried my wife inside me –
like a cable car I pulled her
up the mountainside of our days.

I lifted her quite naturally
and I carried the floating,
prancing seahorse within her.

I took them both to the crossroads.
Stooping like St Christopher
I bore her – a slippery wave.

The hospital parted for us
strongly as the Red Sea.
I coaxed her through swing doors

which gusted to and fro
like our past and future.
She was sea-sick.

Sometimes she could hardly
remember who I was.
I only intended to leave her

for a moment in the bulrushes,
but she slept and slept,
hibernated like a star

gone to ground.
Then I carried her
to the ends of the Earth.

Moniza Alvi

My sun sets to rise again

Robert Browning

FROM THE IRISH

According to Dinneen, a Gael unsurpassed
in lexicographical enterprise, the Irish
for moon means the white circle in a slice
of half-boiled potato or turnip. A star
is the mark on the forehead of a beast
and the sun is the bottom of a lake, or well.

Well, if I say to you your face
is like a slice of half-boiled turnip,
your hair is the colour of a lake's bottom
and at the centre of each of your eyes
is the mark of the beast, it is beacause
I want to love you properly, according to Dinneen.

Ian Duhig

SYMPTOMS

Although you have given me a stomach upset,
Weak knees, a lurching heart, a fuzzy brain,
A high-pitched laugh, a monumental phone bill,
A feeling of unworthiness, sharp pain
When you are somewhere else, a guilty conscience,
A longing, and a dread of what's in store,
A pulse rate for the Guinness Book of Records –
Life now is better than it was before.

Although you have given me a raging temper,
Insomnia, a rising sense of panic,
A hopeless challenge, bouts of introspection,
Raw, bitten nails, a voice that's strangely manic,
A selfish streak, a fear of isolation,
A silly smile, lips that are chapped and sore,
A running joke, a risk, an inspiration –
Life now is better than it was before.

Although you have given me a premonition,
Chattering teeth, a goal, a lot to lose,
A granted wish, mixed motives, superstitions,
Hang-ups and headaches, fear of awful news,
A bubble in my throat, a dare to swallow,
A crack of light under a closing door,
The crude, fantastic prospect of forever –
Life now is better than it was before.

Sophie Hannah

THE INVISIBLE MENDER (My First Mother)

I'm sewing on new buttons
to this washed silk shirt.
Mother of pearl,
I chose them carefully.
In the haberdashers on Chepstow Place
I turned a boxful over
one by one,
searching for the backs with flaws:
those blemished green or pink or aubergine,
small birth marks on the creamy shell.

These afternoons are short,
the sunlight buried after three or four,
sap in the cold earth.
The trees are bare.
I'm six days late.
My right breast aches so
when I bend to catch a fallen button
that strays across the floor.
Either way,
there'll be blood on my hands.

Thirty-seven years ago you sat in poor light
and sewed your time away,
then left.
But I'm no good at this:
a peony of blood gathers on my thumb, falls
then widens on the shirt like a tiny, opening mouth.

I think of you like this -
as darkness comes,
as the window that I can't see through
is veiled with mist
which turns to condensation
slipping down tall panes of glass,
a mirror to the rain outside -
and I know that I'll not know
if you still are mending in the failing light,
or if your hands (as small as mine)
lie still now, clasped together, underground.

Sarah Maguire

WATER COOLER MOMENTS

We shared water cooler moments
Every other other day
Wishful water cooler moments
And they can't take them away
Wry, dry looks that had no witnesses
Rueful smiles and knowing grimaces
I can't prove it, but we shared them
And I like to think you cared then
That you weren't just being nice to me
You sent memos with your eyes to me
And I reciprocated
Though I may have mistranslated
– Meanings added, meanings missed –
I'm pretty sure I got the gist

We didn't ever action
Our un-minuted attraction
We each knew that we shouldn't
So we didn't, though we could, it
Seemed we had an understanding
Or that's how I understood it
Till that moment when you winced at me
Went halfway to convincing me
I'd passed the out-of -order- line
And hovered on the borderline
Between being an embarrassment
And being charged with harassment
And then you merged with Marketing

And now to my intense regret
You use the little kitchenette
That's time-shared with the 2nd floor
A long mile down the corridor
The rest's not even history
There never was a you and me
Though might have been so easily
There's a question that's implicit here
And I admit I'm begging it –
Okay, the word 'relationship'
Pudding-wise, is over-egging it

Re: 'the first stone', let those who've never
Wished and wondered cast it –
It was a beautiful speculationship
While it lasted

Matt Harvey

BECAUSE SHE WOULD ASK ME WHY I LOVED HER

If questioning could make us wise
no eyes would ever gaze in eyes;
if all our tale were told in speech
no mouths would wander each to each.

Were spirits free from mortal mesh
and love not bound in hearts of flesh
no aching breasts would yearn to meet
and find their ecstacy complete.

For who is there that loves and knows
The secret powers by which he grows?
Were knowledge all, what were our need
to thrill and faint and sweetly bleed?

Then seek not, sweet, the *If* and *Why*
I love you now until I die:
For I must love because I live
And life in me is what you give.

Christopher Brennan

INCANTATA
(Excerpt)
In memory of Mary Farl Powers

I thought of you again tonight, thin as a rake, as you bent
over the copper plate of 'Emblements',
its tidal wave of army-worms into which you all but
$$\text{disappeared:}$$
I wanted to catch something of its spirit
and yours, to body out your disembodied *vox
clamantis in deserto,* to let this all-too-cumbersomen device
of a potato-mouth in a potato-face
speak out, unencumbered, from its long, low, mould-filled
$$\text{box}$$

Paul Muldoon

INTERLUDES

Not a beginning, not an end,
this neutral place
is rich with stillness,
with movement in all directions.
In the word of the prophet, we
are travellers. So pass in peace, stranger,
though our orbits differ,
I too have rested here at these
limbo interludes
in our shared planet's rotation.
So catch your breath and let my words
welcome you like a friend's blessing.
May this space around you expand
and glow in the warmth of knowing
that it's only a corridor;
not a beginning, not an end,
but a green oasis.

Debjani Chatterjee

A WHITE ROSE

The red rose whispers of passion,
And the white rose breathes of love;
O, the red rose is a falcon,
And the white rose is a dove.

But I send you a cream-white rosebud
With a flush on its petal tips;
For the love that is purest and sweetest
Has a kiss of desire on the lips.

John Boyle O'Reilly

INVISIBLE KISSES

If there was ever one
Whom when you were sleeping
Would wipe your tears
When in dreams you were weeping;
Who would offer you time
When others demand;
Whose love lay more infinite
Than grains of sand.

If there was ever one
To whom you could cry;
Who would gather each tear
And blow it dry;
Who would offer help
On the mountains of time;
Who would stop to let each sunset
Soothe the jaded mind.

If there was ever one
To whom when you run
Will push back the clouds
So you are bathed in sun;
Who would open arms
If you would fall;
Who would show you everything
If you lost it all.

If there was ever one
Who when you achieve
Was there before the dream
And even then believed;

Who would clear the air
When it's full of loss;
Who would count love
Before the cost.

If there was ever one
Who when you are cold
Will summon warm air
For your hands to hold;
Who would make peace
In pouring pain,
Make laughter fall
In falling rain.

If there was ever one
Who can offer you this and more;
Who in keyless rooms
Can open doors;
Who in open doors
Can see open fields
And in open fields
See harvests yield.

Then see only my face
In the reflection of these tides
Through the clear water
Beyond the river side.
All I can send is love

In all that this is
A poem and a necklace
Of invisible kisses.

Lemn Sissay

THE DARK SIDE OF THE MOON
for Mary

While Markie shunned light and human company,
scrabbled his bulk under the bath in fright,
took to drinking from the toilet bowl, Kitty
would pounce on thistledown, tricks of the light.

Once in a while, I catch them too – is it wind,
slink of a tail in the corner of my eye?
No – only a slippage of time, habit of mind,
a will o' the wisp I could swear shot by.

Low-lying shrubs, shade-loving plants, dry beds
in the valley below and a dull quiet lane
whose shade I hug now draw me downwards,

down to the floorboard dark where illness, pain,
flatten their fur and even sun freaks find
the dark side of the moon is just as kind.

Mimi Khalvati

HOPE IS THE THING WITH FEATHERS

Hope is the thing with feathers
That perches in the soul,
And sings the tune--without the words,
And never stops at all,

And sweetest in the gale is heard;
And sore must be the storm
That could abash the little bird
That kept so many warm.

I've heard it in the chillest land,
And on the strangest sea;
Yet, never, in extremity,
It asked a crumb of me.

Emily Dickinson

I WANNA BE YOURS

I wanna be your vacuum cleaner
breathing in your dust
I wanna be your Ford Cortina
I will never rust
If you like your coffee hot
let me be your coffee pot
You call the shots
I wanna be yours

I wanna be your raincoat
for those frequent rainy days
I wanna be your dreamboat
when you want to sail away
Let me be your teddy bear
take me with you anywhere
I don't care
I wanna be yours

I wanna be your electric meter
I will not run out
I wanna be the electric heater
you'll get cold without
I wanna be your setting lotion
hold your hair in deep devotion
Deep as the deep Atlantic Ocean
That's how deep is my devotion.

John Cooper Clarke

SONG TO CELIA

Drink to me, only with thine eyes
And I will pledge with mine;
Or leave a kiss but in the cup,
And I'll not look for wine.
The thirst that from the soul doth rise
Doth ask a drink divine:
But might I of Jove's nectar sup
I would not change for thine.

I sent thee late a rosy wreath,
Not so much honouring thee
As giving it a hope that there
It could not withered be
But thou thereon didst only breath
send'st it back to me:
Since, when it grows and smells, I swear,
Not of itself but thee.

Ben Jonson

PERFECT DAY

I am just a woman of the shore
wearing your coat against the snow
that falls on the oyster-catcher's tracks
and on our own; falls
on the still grey waters
of Loch Morar, and on our shoulders
gentle as restraint: a perfect weight
of snow as tree-boughs
and fences bear against a loaded sky:
one flake more, they'd break.

Kathleen Jamie

STATELY HOME

The one thing I can recall is
the painted Swedish chair in the playroom,
a heart cut out of its back.
Which is how I feel now
as paint flakes off the gate.

There, on the hall table, would be
my mother's sequined gloves
in love with each other in a pool of light,
the faded purple curtains, the sanity
of doilies. Upstairs, my baby dresses

might lie like pressed flowers
under glass, unvisited,
my five-year-old voice trapped
in the cupboard in which I once
whispered a poem.

Round the back you'd see the sundial
pointing up to the Sychnant Mountain
I longed to climb, when every bedtime
I'd check my piece of driftwood,
still safe under the pillow.

Samantha Wynne-Rhydderch

ENOUGH

(for Karen Aqua)

Animation: *The action of imparting life, vitality, or motion; quickening; inspiration with courage; the technique by means of which movement is given, on film, to a series of drawings. (OED)*

This is your patient magic: time
slicing each second to a fan of frames
where nothing seems to move, and yet
coyote swells to fish and fish to bird
in a turning circle, and something flaps away.

Watch how this innocent bud
stretches and flowers in a pregnant cloud
of nuclear fall-out; watch how the carved gods
shiver, how they leap frantic from the rocks.

You have captured time's shimmer,
the dance of erratic cells
vibrating inside the body like bright beads
stripped from the thread. A three-second sequence
can take you whole days.

I see you on your knees
with a pack of childhood crayons, as you try to catch
corpuscles inching forwards. How much
time do you have? How much
do I, does anyone? *Enough*

to ease these shaded bodies imperceptibly apart
and film them frame by frame,
while the world turns white and logs crumble to ash

then see them dance onscreen in a bright rush.

Susan Wicks

The best portion of a good man's life,
His little, nameless, unremembered acts,
Of kindness and of love.

William Wordsworth

WANTED TO SAY SOMETHING ABOUT
GRANDFATHER

how one white afternoon under the vines
he stripped a cucumber with his penknife, and offered –
but my lecturer told us: *the edifice of consciousness*
needs a scaffold of knowledge

– though my grandfather said
nothing, just walked ahead beneath a bladderwrack of figs
whose rinsed greenish light made me gasp for brilliance
then to a cove of starfish leaves

where he speared some underwater
spiculed thing – a creature that had, it seemed, never
proper sun – and pared it, alive, to near-greenness
in hands cured to leather

by cigar smoke, the earth;
yet in me, still, that bloodless child – winks
at the one full-lit dapple finding my face, at his need
to shave a rind, strip by

translucent strip, holding its last
wet film up to light – that's it: grandfather making light
of the knowing in his eyes – how he saw in me days broad
as a noon-lit road where I see

only a narrow past: that he held out
this – his grandfather's seed – nerving that flesh, running
its length like a glyph through rock – each time I slice
watercolour stars or strike

a salad's strange mint of coins.

Mario Petrucci

What you leave behind is not what is engraved in stone
monuments, but what is woven into the lives of others.

Pericles

LET ME NOT TO THE MARRIAGE OF TRUE MINDS

Let me not to the marriage of true minds
Admit impediments. Love is not love
Which alters when it alteration finds,
Or bends with the remover to remove:
O no! It is an ever-fixed mark
That looks on tempests and is never shaken;
It is the star to every wandering bark,
Whose worth's unknown, although his height be taken.
Love's not Time's fool, though rosy lips and cheeks
Within his bending sickles's compass come:
Love alters not with his brief hours and weeks,
But bears it out even to the edge of doom.
      If this be error and upon me proved,
      I never writ, nor no man ever loved.

William Shakespeare

LULLABY

By candlelight one enters Babylon.
Can you hold it still for me?
I want you to shield its light from Syria
The way you would hide your knowledge from a child.
Pick up your feet like this. Don't cry.
The pain will soon pass.
These merchants are my friends.

Now candles encircle Babylon's ends
One candle is enough
To save us from distortion while we pray.
Please, no more school today!
It's tempting to ask
Why roads that lead to Babylon by night
Encircle her so modestly next day.
But all roads lead to blindness at last
For those who are drawn towards their fate.
What you see
Is all that has been left out for you by the night.
The rest will have to wait.

Now word has passed across the city while you slept
The gatekeeper opens the East Gate
And the sun enters Babylon alone.
Put out the light.
These merchants will show you the way to your house.

Hugo Williams

GALACTIC LOVE POEM
(for Susan)

Warm your feet at the sunset
Before we go to bed
Read your book by the light of Orion
With Sirius guarding your head
Then reach out and switch off the planets
We'll watch them go out one by one
You kiss me and tell me you love me
By the light of the last setting sun
We'll both be up early tomorrow
A new universe has begun.

Adrian Henri

YOUR BREAST IS ENOUGH

Your breast is enough for my heart,
and my wings for your freedom.
What was sleeping above your soul will rise
out of my mouth to heaven.

In you is the illusion of each day.
You arrive like the dew to the cupped flowers.
You undermine the horizon with your absence.
Eternally in flight like the wave.

I have said that you sang in the wind
like the pines and like the masts.
Like them you are tall and taciturn,
and you are sad, all at once, like a voyage.

You gather things to you like an old road.
You are peopled with echoes and nostalgic voices.
I awoke and at times the birds fled and migrated
That had been sleeping in your soul.

Pablo Neruda

LOVE SONG FOR LUCINDA

Love
Is a ripe plum
Growing on a purple tree.
Taste it once
And the spell of its enchantment
Will never let you be.

Love
Is a bright star
Glowing in far Southern skies.
Look too hard
And its burning flame
Will always hurt your eyes.

Love
Is a high mountain
Stark in a windy sky.
If you
Would never lose your breath
Do not climb too high.

Langston Hughes

SILENTIUM AMORIS

As often-times the too resplendent sun
Hurries the pallid and reluctant moon
Back to her sombre cave, ere she hath won
A single ballad from the nightingale,
So doth thy Beauty make my lips to fail,
And all my sweetest singing out of tune.

And as at dawn across the level mead
On wings impetuous some wind will come,
And with its too harsh kisses break the reed
Which was its only instrument of song,
So my too stormy passions work me wrong,
And for excess of Love my Love is dumb.

But surely unto Thee mine eyes did show
Why I am silent, and my lute unstrung;
Else it were better we should part, and go,
Thou to some lips of sweeter melody,
And I to muse the barren memory
Of unkissed kisses, and songs never sung.

Oscar Wilde

HER SPIRIT

Her spirit moves wind chimes
   When air is still
      And fills the rooms
         With fragrance of lily

Her eyes blue green
   Still seen
      Perfectly happy
         With nothing

Her spirit sets
   The water pipes a-humming
      Fat lektronic force be with ya sound

Her spirit talks to me
   Through animals
      Beautiful creature
         Lay with me

Bird that calls my name
   Insists that she is here
      And nothing
         Left to fear

Bright white squirrel
   Foot of tree
      Fixes me
         With innocent gaze

Her spirit talks to me

Sir Paul McCartney

58

COUNTDOWN

Three turns in the corridor
to the anaesthetic room, one last walk
with breasts, the weight of them
familiar as my own name
and address. Slick of the Thames
through plate glass intoxicates.

A young man in a white coat small-talks
London, fixes a cannula into the wrist
where my watch is not. My lips
keep moving – explain we left
some years ago, not the stress,
more the desire to raise our child
on chalk hills, near the sea.

His eyes clear as a newborn's
close to my face, he holds my hand –
a moment of love, I will call it that.
I lend him this life, veins freezing
from the forearm up.

Clare Best

A DAY BY THE SEA AND OTHER STORIES

...c'était une partie de son être qui avait fini d'exister
                    'En famile'. Guy de Maupassant

The windows of the tram car were open
and all the curtains floated in the wind.
I love this book because you gave it to me,
short stories you're too young to understand.

The door opened and Dr Chenet appeared.
On this near-deserted beach I think of you
at home beside the window, playing
on the dark piano that I learned on too.

The windows of the tram car were open.
I swim alone now on a glittering tide
of doctors, clocks and chests of drawers,
gas lamps, free-floating globes of light.

I love this book because you gave it to me.
He thought of his mother in Picardy, just
as she was when he was a boy. Recognisable
people and what happened to them next.

Jane Draycott

THE PRESENT

For the present there is just one moon,
though every level pond gives back another.

But the bright disc shining in the black lagoon,
perceived by astrophysicist and lover,

is milliseconds old. And even that light's
seven minutes older than its source.

And the stars we think we see on moonless nights
are long extinguished. And, of course,

this very moment, as you read this line,
is literally gone before you know it.

Forget the here-and-now. We have no time
but this device of wantoness and wit.

Make me this present then: your hand in mine,
and we'll live out our lives in it.

Michael Donaghy

CITY LILACS

In crack-haunted alleys, overhangs,
plots of sour earth that pass for gardens,
in the space between wall and wheelie bin,
where men with mobiles make urgent conversation,
where bare-legged girls shiver in April winds,
where a new mother stands on her doorstep and blinks
at the brightness of morning, so suddenly born –
in all these places the city lilacs are pushing
their cones of blossom into the spring
to be taken by the warm wind.
Lilac, like love, makes no distinction.
It will open for anyone.
Even before love knows that it is love
lilac knows it must blossom.
In crack-haunted alleys, in overhangs,
in somebody's front garden
abandoned to crisp packets and cans,
on landscaped motorway roundabouts,
in the depths of parks
where men amd women are lost in transactions
of flesh and cash, where mobiles ring
and the deal is done – here the city lilacs
release their sweet, wild perfume
Then blows down, heavy with rain.

Helen Dunmore

THE MAN IN THE STATION

He just appeared: some said he came off a late train, some
thought they'd seen him round town. Others said they heard
he lived on a houseboat on the south side of the city. He wore
a checked shirt and jeans, stained black at the knees, the
bottoms frayed and grimy. He had no shoes. He made his
home on a bench at the far end of the railway station, just
below a concrete ramp, a walk-up to the street above. It was
an exit, but poorly lit and steep, and not many people used it.
So no one noticed him for a while, perhaps. And no one had
noticed the bench before he came; it was so out of the way,
surrounded by broken bottles and cartons and debris blown
off the track. It wasn't the kind of place a person would
choose to sit. There was a straggling buddleia bush to his left;
the blackened brick wall of the terminus to his right; the
tracks straight ahead. A woman who lived on the street above
was the first to notice him; at least, the first to talk to him.
She asked if he needed anything, but the man shook his head.
She was very old and he was young, and she was reminded of
her grandson, she said, who once got stuck at Liverpool
Street station overnight because he'd lost his ticket and didn't
have enough money to buy another. Afterwards she would
remark on how thin he was. A few days later, in the early
morning, a builder on a job in the area passed him and placed
a packet of biscuits on the bench. Someone else left a pint of
milk, another some soup in a flask.

The bench became filled with offerings: chocolate bars
and tins of pop and sandwiches wrapped in foil; and - perhaps
because the man never touched these items - others began to

leave less perishable gifts; a blanket, a book, a small portable radio, a child's torch. Someone had hung a rosary off a branch of the buddleia, which had begun to bloom.

By the time the paramedics were called, the man was lying on his side; had been on his side and not moving for a couple of days. The woman on the street above had called them. The paramedics stayed with him for a while, feeling the heat of the sun and watching the butterflies flitter around their heads, but the man wanted nothing, and there was nothing they could do. They came back the next day, called this time by the builder, who said the man had died. They didn't find him, but a fine coating remained on the surface of the bench, sparkling in the sunlight like gold dust.

The old woman started a collection for a plaque to put on the bench, nothing ostentatious, just to mark his passing; she pinned a notice on the lamp-post requesting donations. By now the buddleia was ornamented with offerings from people who had seen him, people who had heard of him, people who had no idea what the memorial was for, but felt the need to leave something: real flowers and silk flowers, ribbons of various colours, a framed photograph of a loved-one, a prayer card, a pair of baby shoes. Many of these people contributed to the fund, dropping their donations through the old woman's letterbox.

The rail authority posted an official letter over hers; a litter abatement notice. When the old woman complained, a man in a uniform pointed out that it was not a bench at all, simply a pair of railway sleepers stacked one upon the other, and that, though they were sympathetic, littering was an offence punishable by law.

No one saw them remove the bench, chop down the buddleia, take away the offerings. But the old woman saw, the following summer, what had replaced them. She stared down in wonder at the spot where he had been, and saw a bright golden haze, a cluster of Aaron's rod, shimmering in the sun like a thousand butterflies.

Trezza Azzopardi

IMPROMPTU TO MISS UTRECIA SMITH
On her not dancing, 1743

Whilst round in wild rotations hurl'd,
These glittering forms I view,
Methinks the busy restless world
Is pictured in a few.
So may the busy world advance,
Since thus the Fates decree,
It still may have its busy dance,
Whilst I retire with thee.

William Shenstone

I LUV ME MUDDER

I luv me mudder an me mudder luvs me
    We cum so far from over de sea,
We heard dat de streets were paved wid gold
    Sometimes it's hot, sometimes it's cold,
I luv me mudder an me mudder luvs me
    We try fe live in harmony
Yu might know her as Valerie
    But to me she's just my mummy.

She shouts at me daddy so loud sometime
    She's always been a friend of mine
She's always doing de best she can
    She works so hard down ina Englan,
She's always singin sum kinda song
    She has big muscles an she very, very strong,
She likes pussycats an she luvs cashew nuts
    An she don't bother wid no if an buts.

I luv me mudder an me mudder luvs me
    We come so far from over de sea,
We heard dat de streets were paved wid gold
    Sometimes it's hot, sometimes it's cold,
I luv her and whatever we do
    Dis a love I know is true,
My people, I'm talking to yu
    Me an my mudder we luv yu too.

Benjamin Zephaniah

CHLORIS IN THE SNOW

I saw fair Chloris walk alone
When feather'd rain came softly down,
As Jove descending from his Tower
To court her in a silver shower:
The wanton snow flew to her breast,
Like pretty birds into their nest,
But overcome with whiteness there,
For grief it thawed into a tear;
Thence falling on her garment's hem
To deck her, froze into a gem.

William Strode

FATHER TO SON
for Matthew

No one would know, unless they actually knew –
Or even notice the drab brown building facing
The Apollo supermarket. Once inside,
Traffic noise on the odd branch waving from
Beyond the window are insufficient distractions
From evidence which multiplies in folders,
Time that aches and aches in clinic queues
And the outraged screams of children.

Each time we go, my heart begins to sink
Almost as much as yours must – most of all
When we first glimpse, beyond a door, then confront
Those alien machines, grotesque or sleek,
Whose circuits you, their missing part, must complete.
With all their tubes, dials, monitors and screens,
We have to trust them as benign, despite
The pain they may also bring.

Beyond all this – the caring smiles and skills
Of nurses and radiographers, and the doctors
So famous that, jet-lagged they have to ring
In from the airport to give the go-ahead
For pre-meds; beyond the knowledge, too, that others
Are suffering more – a part of you still craves
A chance to reject it all.

And part of me, confounded by love and fear,
Would almost sign a pact as your accomplice –
Anything rather than more tinkering to cope

With a defect no one can help. Almost - forgive
That qualifying doubt whose other side
Is hope. Beyond a certain point of bruising
Neither can talk of this.

Lawrence Sail

If I have seen further it is by
standing on the shoulders of giants.

Sir Isaac Newton

MAY YOU ALWAYS HAVE AN ANGEL BY
YOUR SIDE

May you always have an angel by your side
Watching out for you
Helping you believe in brighter days and in dreams come true
Giving you comfort and courage
Someone to catch you if you fall
Inspiring smiles
Holding your hand and helping you through it all
May you always have an angel by your side

Douglas Pagels

SUDDEN LIGHT

I have been here before,
    But when or how I cannot tell:
I know the grass beyond the door,
    The sweet keen smell,
The sighing sound, the lights around the shore.

You have been mine before, -
    How long ago I may not know:
But just when that swallow's soar
    Your neck turned so,
Some veil did fall, - I knew it all of yore.

Has this been thus before?
    And shall not thus time's eddying flight
Still with our lives our love restore
    In death's despite,
And day and night yield one delight once more?

Dante Gabriel Rossetti

SHE WALKS IN BEAUTY LIKE THE NIGHT

She walks in beauty, like the night
Of cloudless climes and starry skies,
And all that's best of dark and bright
Meets in her aspect and her eyes;
Thus mellow'd to that tender light
Which Heaven to gaudy day denies.

One shade the more, one ray the less,
Had half impair'd the nameless grace
Which waves in every raven tress
Or softly lightens o'er her face,
Where thoughts serenely sweet express
How pure, how dear their dwelling-place.

And on that cheek and o'er that brow
So soft, so calm, yet eloquent,
The smiles that win, the tints that glow,
But tell of days in goodness spent, –
A mind at peace with all below,
A heart whose love is innocent.

Lord Byron

SEPIA ROADS

We can no longer
Brush away tears
Which have etched themselves
Into fleshlines,
Nor load the bristle
With the brilliant tones
Of our first embrace.
Now that the oaks have grown
And we stand
A little smaller in their shade,
Fumbling for
Each other's hand;
Over painting
Deeper sepia roads.

Chris Tutton

THE TRANS-SIBERIAN EXPRESS
(For Eva)

One day we will make our perfect journey –
the great train smashing through Dundee, Brooklyn
and off into the endless tundra,
the earth flattening out before us,

I follow your continuous arrival,
shedding veil after veil after veil –
the automatic doors wincing away
while you stagger back from the buffet

slopping *Laphroaig* and decent coffee
until you face me from that long enfilade
of glass, stretched to vanishing point
like facing mirrors, a lifetime of days.

Don Paterson

LEISURE

What is this life if, full of care,
We have no time to stand and stare.
No time to stand beneath the boughs
And stare as long as sheep or cows.
No time to see, when woods we pass,
Where squirrels hide their nuts in grass.
No time to see, in broad daylight,
Streams full of stars, like skies at night.
No time to turn at Beauty's glance,
And watch her feet, how they can dance.
No time to wait till her mouth can
Enrich that smile her eyes began.
A poor life this if, full of care,
We have no time to stand and stare.

W H Davies

CUTTING THE POPULATION

I remember that day in the barber's
When Patrick's dad was there
He took something for the weekend
And left behind some hair,

And though I was of tender years
I knew for Roman Catholics
That something for the weekend
Should be church not prophylactics,

I sat and had my hair cut
And thought of Patrick's dad
And thought of Patrick's mother
And how much sex they had,

Was it just at weekends
When the pair would get it on?
And was it just at weekends
When half his hair had gone?

And then I thought of Patrick
And his brothers Phil and Steve
His sisters Jane and Catherine
Not forgetting Gill and Eve

It seemed that on most weekends
Patrick's dad was getting hot
And it didn't really matter
If his hair was cut or not.

Marvin Cheeseman

YORKSHIRE PUDDING RULES

The tin must not gleam. Must never be new.
If there is dried sweat somewhere in its metal
It must be your mother's. The flour must be strong
And white as the face of Uncle Jack
When he came back from the desert. The eggs
Must come from an allotment. The allotment
Must belong to yout father-in-law.
The eggs have to be broken
With one swift movement over the bowl.
If there is dried sweat somewhere in its Pyrex
It must be your mother's. The milk
Must have been delivered by Colin Leech
at 04.30. The fork has to be an old one. The wrist
Must, simply must, ache after the mixing.
The flour must introduce itself to the yolk of the egg.
The egg has to be allowed to talk to the flour.
The milk must dance with them both: foxtrot then quickstep.
The pepper must be scatterd, black on off-white.
The oven must be hotter than ever.
The lard has to come in a tight white pack.
The lard must almost catch fire in the oven.
The oven door must open and you must shout
JESUS CHRIST as the heat smacks you in the chops.

Follow these rules
And the puddings will rise to heaven
And far beyond.

Ian McMillan

THE FULMAR

I watch the fulmar hurl its breast
To the wind's unseen geometry;
Spread wings on nothing, reckless of gravity,
And ride that risk
And rest
On sheer uncertainty,

Choosing no choice.

I must learn to be like him,
To follow the reach and search of air –
Swoop, sink, stand, balance, soar on the invisible spiral stair–
And not resist
But trust,
And be carried there.

Katrina Porteous

A VISIT

I still remember love like another country
        with an almost forgotten landscape
of salty skin and a dry mouth. I think
        there was always a temptation to escape
from the violence of that sun, the sudden
        insignificance of ambition,
the prowl of jealousy like a witch's cat.

    Last night I was sailing in my sleep
        like an old seafarer, with scurvy
colouring my thoughts, there was moonlight
        and ice on green waters.
Hallucinations. Dangerous nostalgia.
        And early this morning you whispered
as if you were lying softly at my side:

Are you still angry with me? And spoke my
        name with so much tenderness, I cried.
I never reproached you much
        that I remember, not even when I should;
to me, you were the boy in Ravel's garden
        who always longed to be good,
as the forest creatures knew, and so do I.

Elaine Feinstein

BENEATH MY HANDS

Beneath my hands
your small breasts
are the upturned bellies
of breathing fallen sparrows.

Wherever you move
I hear the sounds of closing wings
of falling wings.

I am speechless
because you have fallen beside me
because your eyelashes
are the spines of tiny fragile animals.

I dread the time
when your mouth
begins to call me hunter.

When you call me close
to tell me
your body is not beautiful
I want to summon
the eyes and hidden mouths
of stone and light and water
to testify against you.

I want them
to surrender before you
the trembling rhyme of your face
from their deep caskets.

When you call me close
to tell me
your body is not beautiful
I want my body and my hands
to be pools
for your looking and laughing.

Leonard Cohen

LOVE SONG

If I could write words
Like leaves on an Autumn forest floor,
What a bonfire my letters would make.

If I could speak words of water,
You would drown when I said
"I love you."

Spike Milligan

HIMALAYAN BALSAM

Orchid-lipped, loose-jointed, purplish, indolent flowers,
with a ripe smell of peaches, like a girl's breath through
                                            lipstick,
delicate and coarse in the weedlap of late summer rivers,
dishevelled, weak-stemmed, common as brambles, as love
                                            which

subtracts us from seasons, their courtships and murders,
(*Meta segmentata* in her web, and the male waiting,
between blossom and violent blossom, meticulous spiders
repeated in gossamer, and the slim males waiting).

Fragrance too rich for keeping, too light to remember,
like grief for the cat's sparrow and the wild gull's
beach-hatched embryo. (She ran from the reaching water
with the broken egg in her hand, but the clamped bill

refused brandy and grubs, a shred too naked and perilous for
life, offered freely in cardboard boxes, little windowsill
coffins for bird death, kitten death, squirrel death, summer
repeated and ended in heartbreak, in sad small funerals.)

Sometimes, shaping bread or scraping potatoes for supper,
I have stood in the kitchen, transfixed by what I'd call love,
if love were a whiff, a wanting for no particular lover,
no child, or baby, or creature. 'Love, dear love,'

I could cry to these scent-spilling ragged flowers,
and mean nothing but 'no', in that word's breath,
to their evident going, their important descent through
                                            red towering
stalks to the riverbed. It's not, as I thought, that death

82

creates love. More that love knows death. Therefore
tears, therefore poems, therefore long stone sobs of cathedrals
that speak to no ferret or fox, that prevent no massacre.
(I am combing abundant leaves from these icy shallows.)

Love, it was you who said 'Murder the killer
we have to call life and we'd be a bare planet under a dead
                                                    sun.'
Then I loved you with the usual soft lust of October
That says 'yes' to the coming winter and a summoning odour
                                                    of balsam.

Anne Stevenson

THE WHITE BIRDS

I would that we were, my beloved, white birds on the foam of
the sea!
We tire of the flame of the meteor, before it can fade and flee;
And the flame of the blue star of twilight, hung low on the
rim of the sky,
Has awakened in our hearts, my beloved, a sadness that may
not die.

A weariness comes from those dreamers, dew-dabbled, the
lily and rose;
Ah, dream not of them, my beloved, the flame of the meteor
that goes,
Or the flame of the blue star that lingers hung low in the fall
of the dew:
For I would we were changed to white birds on the wandering
foam, I and you!

I am haunted by numberless islands and many a Danaan
shore,
Where Time would surely forget us, and Sorrow come near
us no more;
Soon far from the rose and the lily, and fret of the flames
would we be,
Were we only white birds, my beloved, buoyed out on the
foam of the sea!

W B Yeats

CHARMS FOR LOVE

from the traditional Romanian

I beat you with a hazel rod
Come to me in madness

I beat you with a bloodied rod
Come like an angel

I beat you with a rod from heaven
Come to me like a wild boar

*

Ninety-nine serpents –
ninety-nine flaming beasts –
go to Ion
Slip in by his shirt-collar
squat in his heart
scald him burn him
turn his eyes to my eyes
his face to my face
his path to my house
Make him see me in the distance
a fine-feathered peacock
make him pick me out as basil among weeds
make him tease me of all the girls
As you follow gold and silver
fall in step with my words
with my walk
with my dance

*

Sweet boy
don't send so much longing –
send a little less
and come with it yourself

*

Tuesday, basket full of black,
how did you make me fall in love –
did you clip my hair
did you steal my footsteps?
How did you charm me –
With the hair of a mad wolf
with three straws from the bed
with splintered wood
with the fairness of eyebrows
with a chip off the gate
with a dark hair from a braid?
How did you drive every other love away?

*

Eagle, my eaglet, grow into a flying bird
Take yourself to Ion's house
What you find in his head
take in your head
what you find in his ears
take in your ears
what you find in his mouth
take in your mouth

what you find in his hands
take in your wings
Take that great wrong away in your feathers –

and what you find in your head
put it in her head
And what you find in your feathers
put it on the table
in their house

Fiona Sampson

SNOWDROPS

As I stare at the small
white heads, their circular bed
set in a bald frontage,
the afternoon swells
with distress. I imagine picking,
imagine pressing layers
of green-rimmed petals
to my chest to cover
the emptiness which will shout
when I lose my left breast.

Though they look weak
beneath a bush's crude
black spread of branches
these are not drops, crystals,
bells that ring thinly,
not hangdog ninnies,
timid girls running out of breath.

They have heaved through
weighty clay lumps,
speared freezing air
to bloom without summer's prop -
are more daring
fiercer than the swimming
open-mouthed fear that wants
to devour me. They stand

uncowed by the north wind,
its sudden bluster, cruel bite.
And as I move on each flower
fills me like an annunciation.

Myra Schneider

HAIKU

laughter lines –
the scar around my breast
faded now

Lynne Rees

COUNTING

You count the fingers first: it's traditional.
(You assume the doctor counted them too,
when he lifted up the slimy surprise
with its long dark pointed head and its father's nose
at 2.13 a.m. – 'Look at the clock!'
said Sister: 'Remember the time: 2.13.')

Next day the head's turned pink and round;
the nose is a blob. You fumble under the gown
your mother embroidered with a sprig of daisies,
as she embroidered your own Viyella gowns
when you were a baby. You fish out
curly triangular feet. You count the toes.

'There's just one little thing' says Sister:
'His ears – they don't quite match. One
has an extra whorl in it. No one will notice.'
You notice like mad. You keep on noticing.
Then you hear a rumour: a woman in the next ward
has had a stillbirth. Or was it something worse?

You lie there, bleeding gratefully.
You've won the Nobel Prize, and the VC,
and the State Lottery, and gone to heaven.
Feed-time comes. They bring your bundle –
the right one: it's him all right.
You count his eyelashes: the ideal number.

You take him home. He learns to walk.
From time to time you eye him,
nonchalantly, from each side.
He has an admirable nose.
No one ever notices his ears. No one
ever stands on both sides of him at once.

He grows up. He has beautiful children.

Fleur Adcock

Who travels for love finds a thousand miles not
longer than one.

Japanese Proverb

SUCKLE
after Frida Kahlo

In my white baby smock
I'm pristine as a glacier.

My nurse is Mexico –
one breast is Popocatépetl

the other, Lake Xochimilco.
I can't look at her mask

as she carries me into the studio
to paint the world tenderly

like a wise baby. I work
at the speed of light.

My ear opens its canal
to listen for the hunger-cry

perched like an insect
on swamp water, the trembling

rings of earth's throat –
when I finish those baby lips

so they can suckle.

Pascale Petit

WOMEN RUNNING

after Picasso: Deux femmes courant sur la plage

Look how their large bodies leaping
from dresses fill the beach, how their breasts
swing happiness, how the mediterraneans
of sea and sky fondle their flesh. Nothing

could rein them in. The blown wildnesses
of their dark animal hair, their hands joined
and raised, shout triumph. All their senses
are roused as they hurtle towards tomorrow.

That arm laid across the horizon,
the racing legs, an unstoppable quartet, pull
me from my skin and I become one of them,
believe I'm agile enough to run a mile,

believe I'm young again, believe age
has been stamped out. No wonder, I worship
at the altar of energy, not the energy huge
with hate which revels in tearing apart,

in crushing to dust but the momentum
which carries blood to the brain, these women
across the plage, lovers as they couple
and tugs at the future till it breaks into bloom.

Myra Schneider

REMOTE
for Zélie

All at once the hours –
alongside stillness
of your curled cat,
now you're not here,

pricks to attention
up-eared at the mere
flick back to dim
of the stereo dial –

Monteverdi's spent
breath folding back
from the aether
and packed into binary

all by the sleight
of my hand, gun –
slinging the remote
that with a glance

of a wavelength
strokes the sensor
and there's hush
for the world to flow into,

the tish tush of rain
that's been battering gusts
all your first night away
in a hospital bed and now

drops to a grey
limp a.m. which a—
mazingly can quicken
with a click,

a cat's twitch, all
ears, all attention
and already
up for it...

Philip Gross

i m Frances Horovitz (1938-1983)

Long gone halcyon

days shine still in love's sweet song

—Your poems, your voice—

Michael Horovitz

TIMES WHEN I DREAM

You arrived. The hills were as they had ever been.
Trees marched up the contours of the land, hiding clearings,
stories in moss.
After a barely warm day, the sun was a fragile coin of
                                                    Honesty
clouds had been driven off, pushed to the edges of the sky
what remained was a dance floor, huge and blue.

Down the valley two dogs answered each other. The weather
                                                    vane,
a crow, creaked to the West, then was still.
In the oven a lasagne came alive – a bubble of layers mixing
                                            cream and blood
a few stars disintegrated, fell to the table. In the dregs of my
                                            glass, a forecast.
I had expected simply to enjoy the wine, a meal, some talk
                                            about books.

Roz Goddard

THE FIRST DAY

I wish I could remember the first day,
First hour, first moment of your meeting me;
If bright or dim the season, it might be
Summer or Winter for aught I can say.
So unrecorded did it slip away,
So blind was I to see and to foresee,
So dull to mark the budding of my tree
That would not blossom yet for many a May.
If only I could recollect it! Such
A day of days! I let it come and go
As traceless as a thaw of bygone snow.
It seemed to mean so little, meant so much!
If only now I could recall that touch,
First touch of hand in hand! – Did one but know!

Christina Rossetti

INCANTATA
(Excerpt)
In memory of Mary Farl Powers

You must have known already, as we moved from the 'Hurly
                                                    Burly'
to McDaid's or Riley's,
that something was amiss: I think you even mentioned a
                                            homeopath
as you showed off the great new acid-bath
in the Graphic Studio, and again undid your portfolio
to lay out your latest works; I try to imagine the strain
you must have been under, pretending to be right as rain
while hearing the bells of a church from some long-flooded
                                                    valley.

From the Quabbin reservoir, maybe, where the banks and
                                            bakeries
of a dozen little submerged Pompeii reliquaries
still do a roaring trade: as clearly as I saw your death-mask
in that swallow's nest, you must have heard the music
rise from the muddy ground between
your breasts as a nocturne, maybe, by John Field;
to think that you thought yourself so invulnerable, so
                                            inviolate,
that a little cancer could be beaten.

Paul Muldoon

SONG

The weight of the world
is love.
Under the burden
of solitude,
under the burden
of dissatisfaction

the weight,
the weight we carry
is love.

Who can deny?
In dreams
it touches
the body,
in thought
constructs
a miracle,
in imagination
anguishes
till born
in human- -
looks out of the heart
burning with purity- -
for the burden of life
is love,

but we carry the weight
wearily,
and so must rest
in the arms of love

at last,
must rest in the arms
of love.

No rest
without love,
no sleep
without dreams
of love- -
be mad or chill
obsessed with angels
or machines,
the final wish
is love
- - cannot be bitter,
cannot deny,
cannot withhold
if denied:

The weight is too heavy

- - must give
for no return
as thought
is given
in solitude
in all the excellence
of its excess.

The warm bodies
shine together
in the darkness,
the hand moves

to the center
of the flesh,
the skin trembles
in happiness
and the soul comes
joyful to the eye- -

Yes, yes,
that's what
I wanted,
I always wanted,
I always wanted,
to return
to the body
where I was born.

Allen Ginsberg

DEATH IS SMALLER THAN I THOUGHT

My Mother and Father died some years ago
I loved them very much.
When they died my love for them
Did not vanish or fade away.
It stayed just about the same,
Only a sadder colour.
And I can feel their love for me,
Same as it ever was.

Nowadays, in good times or bad,
I sometimes ask my Mother and Father
To walk beside me or sit with me
So we can talk together
Or be silent.

They always come to me.
I talk to them and listen to them
And think I hear them talk to me.
It's very simple –
Nothing to do with spiritualism
Or religion or mumbo jumbo.

It is imaginary. It is real. It is love.

Adrian Mitchell

AFTER THE MRI

Driving home from the hospital,
you say, *Those clouds have a gold lining.*

I look up, and it's true,
but I don't want to think about it.

Instead I see myself going to the shops
and coming home too late;

or waking beside you one morning
and thinking you're asleep,

I want to be with you in this, but I'm not:
if I lose you you lose more.

Tomorrow we'll know everything,
you say, and turn to me with a smile.

Henry Shukman

CLOUD & FACE
for a newborn boy

again vaporous
each shifting at inner
strata: chemical energies

as strategy to draw milk
to lips or eyes to
dark under

−rind half−
expecting lightning
to dart earthward bearing

something new − though this
latter light eased &
lengthened

from its bolts
grown gentler with
afternoon gives one brief

smile westward: parting
pink cloud onto
milky

anterior
− for this small
honest breath of the new

boy on the world-block
who looks &
looks

as we do
hoping
to see

Mario Petrucci

Golden slumbers kiss your eyes
Smiles awake you when you rise

Thomas Dekker

A RED, RED ROSE

O my Luve's like a red, red rose,
That's newly sprung in June.
O my Luve's like the melodie,
That's sweetly play'd in tune.

As fair art thou, my bonnie lass,
So deep in luve am I;
And I will luve thee still, my dear,
Till a' the seas gang dry.

Till a' the seas gang dry, my dear,
And the rocks melt wi' the sun,
And I will luve thee still, my dear,
While the sands o' life shall run.

And fare-thee-weel, my only Luve!
And fare-thee-weel, a while!
And I will come again, my Luve,
Tho' 'twere ten thousand mile!

Robert Burns

HOW DO I LOVE THEE?

How do I love thee? Let me count the ways.
I love thee to the depth and breadth and height
My soul can reach, when feeling out of sight
For the ends of Being and ideal Grace.
I love thee to the level of every day's
Most quiet need, by sun and candlelight.
I love thee freely, as men strive for Right;
I love thee purely, as they turn from Praise.
I love thee with the passion put to use
In my old griefs, and with my childhood's faith.
I love thee with a love I seemed to lose
With my lost saints. I love thee with the breath,
Smiles, tears, of all my life! and, if God choose,
I shall but love thee better after death.

Elizabeth Barrett Browning

THE BURNING HOUSE

When a single thought recurring caught
like paper under magnified sunlight,

it didn't take long till flames licked their lips
and devoured windowsill, curtains, chair;

the whole room blackening into one
enormous grate. The towers of books were a gift,

tumbling into clips from the end of the world;
all the words incinerated till nothing

was left of Babel but grey flakes
of lost imaginings. The stairs turned

into the scales of an orange dragon
and the chimney roared. Last to go was the bed,

its mattress resisting the familiar heat,
proud of its memory of metaphor,

its love for play. In the end, even it was
powerless.
By morning all that remained were shadows,

coils of wire. This is what I came home to;
for the first time felt air open through me, pure

as the water that couldn't put the fire out,
strong as the earth deep in my bones.

Linda France

FROM THE ISLAND AT THE EDGE OF THE WORLD

When the north wind sharpens his spears
and the reeds clatter in the marshlands
and the rosemary's blue has been stripped
and all night, instead of the communal chatter
of jackdaws at the chimney your companions
are only the lonely calls of geese migrating away
from this place, and the rattle of stones like loose
teeth in the ebbtide, and you are bone-chilled

Then it's time to listen to the deeper silence
with its undertow of small and timeless voices
that remind you that when you get to the edge
you can choose to keep on walking into night
so that you may finally meet your truer self
coming back the other way, coming home.

Roselle Angwin

IF

If only I could light up your smile like Oprah,
enrapture your soul like Queen Latifah,
say a little prayer for you like Aretha,
make your caged bird rise and sing like Maya.
If I could slide back your blind like Cilla.
and know that you just care for me like Nina,
lend wings to love's javelin like Tessa,
make your head turn, heart flip over like Diana.
If I could spice up your life like Ginger,
add advantage to love like Martina,
set fire to your cigar like Monica,
make fierce erotic-ah like Madonna,
I'd become Uma, Ursula, Ulrika,
your Angela, your Barbra, your chaka.

Patience Agbabi

ULTRASOUND

But I only looked at the screen
when the doctor asked the nurse –
freeze that, will you?

And saw a smoky sea roaring
silently inside my breast,
a kneading ocean of echo-scape,

resonant-surge of sombre waves,

like the Falmouth sea
at autumn twilight, smudge
of grey surfs and bruise-black billows,

grainy shadow-sea inside me,
soundless thump
of seismic wave after wave

breaking over two black rocks,
harmless cysts,

and below, mute, storm-bleak,
the long black trembling scarp of suspect tissue.

Penelope Shuttle

OLD LOVE

In the glance of a mirror, I saw a timid shape
standing in the bevelled bit,
the thin prismatic strip on the edge of the frame
and thought it was a ghost of you.

What are you doing here?
You can't just appear, without warning,
like we were used to it being.
You seemed blurry, like the first and the last time.
In between, how huge you were.
The shadow you cast let much sleep beneath its shade.
You wavered in the air, vanishing.
How I wanted to hold out my hand,
so that your sad ghost
could crawl into a friendly cradle.
Of course it was nothing - a trick of the light
and a splinter in the eye
of a hair gummed across the heart.

No, you are frozen where you were that last time,
deaf and dumb,
a wax-work in the pin-hole museum,
while your tiny, passionate soul,
marooned in the middle of nowhere,
cries and stretches out its arms.

Meanwhile, on my own rock,
on the other side of the world,
I think of you, blind and stumbling in the dark,
while the rescuers throw the beams of their torches
into the wrong cave.

Francesca Beard

QUATRAIN 73

Ah Love! Could thou and I with Fate conspire
To Grasp this sorry scheme of Things entire,
    Would not we shatter it to bits- - and then
Re-mould it nearer to the Heart's Desire!

From The Rubaiyat of Omar Khayyam
Translated by Edward Fitzgerald

THE ELDERBRIDES

It was the day
She first noticed
Her breasts growing.

She sat on the summer-house step;
Felt them tilt
Through her slip.

They shook
Under the cambric,
White does in shade.

It was then
She smelled the elderflower;
The gypsy-blooms,

The rank-dreamers
Who shake out shawls
For the dead.

They trembled above her head,
Five-petalled, five-stamened,
Vibrant in the breeze,

And suffused her body,
Fleeting, equivocal,
In bridal with the stealing sun.

Pauline Stainer

SELF-PORTRAIT WITHOUT BREASTS

Tangled hair, charcoal-socket eyes,
mouth slack after one more long night
restless on my back. This body's fenscape –
manscaped, hills removed – the meaty joins
still livid, tight shut mouths
where distant territories were stitched

in touch. Blood seeps in deltas over ribs,
yellow and purple track to the waist.
You're even more beautiful now, you say
and I believe, for though I never was, I am
explorer, seeker – I've travelled
and I have an ear for truth.

Clare Best

GRACE

A swan pauses in its glide
lifts its head
then
wings hoist wide
launches
a flapping flat-footed furious neck out sprint
the length of the lake

where
in the far reaches
it subsides
composed

as you surface

dimly in corridors
or on your knees

such dogged grace
your beads stilled in your fist
your whispering continuous

you who never broke a vow
still dream of flight, still hope for grace.

Ann Sansom

VALENTINE

Not a red rose or a satin heart.

I give you an onion.
It is a moon wrapped in brown paper.
It promises light
like the careful undressing of love.

Here.
It will blind you with tears
like a lover.
It will make your reflection
a wobbling photo of grief.

I am trying to be truthful.

Not a cute card or a kissogram.

I give you an onion.
Its fierce kiss will stay on your lips,
possessive and faithful
as we are,
for as long as we are.

Take it.
Its platinum loops shrink to a wedding-ring,
if you like.

Lethal.
Its scent will cling to your fingers,
cling to your knife.

Carol Ann Duffy

WARNING

When I am an old woman I shall wear purple
With a red hat which doesn't go, and doesn't suit me.
And I shall spend my pension on brandy and summer gloves
And satin sandals, and say we've no money for butter.
I shall sit down on the pavement when I'm tired
And gobble up samples in shops and press alarm bells
And run my stick along the public railings
And make up for the sobriety of my youth.
I shall go out in my slippers in the rain
And pick the flowers in other people's gardens
And learn to spit.

You can wear terrible shirts and grow more fat
And eat three pounds of sausages at a go
Or only bread and pickle for a week
And hoard pens and pencils and beermats and things in
                                                    boxes.

But now we must have clothes that keep us dry
And pay our rent and not swear in the street
And set a good example for the children.
We must have friends to dinner and read the papers.

But maybe I ought to practise a little now?
So people who know me are not too shocked and surprised
When suddenly I am old, and start to wear purple.

Jenny Joseph

BARRY AND FREDA

Freda and Barry sat one night
The sky was clear, the stars were bright
The wind was soft, the moon was up
Freda drained her cocoa cup
She licked her lips, she felt sublime
She switched off Gardeners Question Time
Barry cringed in fear and dread
As Freda grabbed his tie and said...

Let's do it/Let's do it
Do it while the mood is right
I'm feeling, appealing, I've really got an appetite
I'm on fire, with desire,
I could handle half the tenors in a male voice choir
Let's do it, Let's do it tonight.

BUT HE SAID
I can't do it, can't do it –
I'm not exactly Russell Brand
You're thwarted, I'm sorted
Got my evening's telly planned
It's a pity
The nitty gritty
I've taped eleven episodes of Holby City
Can't do it, can't do it tonight.

SO SHE SAID
Let's do it, let's do it
Do it till our hearts go boom
Go native, creative
Living in the living room

119

This folly, is jolly
Bend me over backwards on my hostess trolley
Let's do it, let's do it tonight.

BUT HE SAID
Can't do it, can't do it -
My heavy breathing days have gone
Niagara, viagra
Nothing really turns me on
Stop stewing
Boo hooing
I've had a good look down there and there's nothing doing.
Can't do it. Can't do it tonight.

SO SHE SAID
Let's do it, let's do it
While I'm really in the mood
Three cheers, it's years,
Since I caught you even semi nude
Get drastic, gymnastic,
Wear your baggy Y-fronts with the loose elastic
Let's do it, let's do it tonight.

I can't do it, can't do it
It's really not my cup of tea.
I'm harassed, embarrased,
I wish you hadn't picked on me.
Don't choose me, don't use me
My mother's sent a note to say you must excuse me
Can't do it, can't do it tonight.

Let's do it, let's do it
I feel I absolutely must

I won't exempt you, want to tempt you
I want to drive you mad with lust
No cautions, just contortions,
Smear an avocado on my lower portions
Let's do it, let's do it tonight.

I can't do it. I can't do it
I must refuse to get unzipped
I'm tearful, I'm fearful
Worried that I'm ill-equipped
Don't bully, I can't fully
Guarantee to cope without a rope and pulley.
Can't do it, can't do it tonight.

Let's do it, let's do it
I really want to run amok
Let's wiggle, let's jiggle, let's really make the rafters rock

Be mighty,
Be flighty,
Come and melt the buttons on my flame-proof nightie
Let's handle
Some scandal
Come and sip Ribena from my peep toe sandal

Not bleakly.
Not meekly.
Beat me on the bottom with a Woman's Weekly

Let's do it
Let's do it
Tonight!

Victoria Wood

STAR LIGHT, STAR BRIGHT

Star, that gives a gracious dole,
What am I to choose?
Oh, will it be a shriven soul,
Or little buckled shoes?

Shall I wish a wedding-ring,
Bright and thin and round,
Or plead you send me covering –
A newly spaded mound?

Gentle beam, shall I implore
Gold, or sailing-ships,
Or beg I hate forevermore
A pair of lying lips?

Swing you low or high away,
Burn you hot or dim;
My only wish I dare not say –
Lest you should grant me him.

Dorothy Parker

BIOPSY

Remote as Venus,
my fiery surface
is probed and surveyed,
samples are taken

Do not worry,
this is science, says someone
Why would I worry?
Stars are not only

above me
but within me,
a firmament,
a shine of bright ones,

milky way of cells
budding and being
and flying along
the body-paths of light and flesh –

In sickness and in health,
I dwell on the planet of love

Penelope Shuttle

SWALLOWS ON THE ISLAND

This early morning again into our small space of air
Like thoughts from nowhere from across salt water
The swallows arrive, voracious, and like the imagination's
Sudden joyous connectings fall to feeding

And the hunted dots of life like invisible particles
Or galaxies are sprung into proved existence
By the turbulence they engender in the visible
Hunters. All that is there. All that food. To think like that

Razor-quick, let alone body out of the hurrying idea
On wings so pointedly how much more hungry than I am
Must I become? The thing in view, they seem by a force of
Their own making to be fended clear of hedges, rocks,

Posts, the rooted tree, the placid horse and in the pack
Of their own kind never hit against another
But each stitches alone in three dimensions, all
In concert making a work your retina cannot hold

Still or the brain fathom. But what you can observe
And try to get the hang of is again and again their splitting
The second on a hesitation before an upwards, down
Or slant new departure, that, the gap in a rhythm,

Space (one of their heartbeats) between a then
And a next, watch closely. They will not stay. A couple of
                                                            days
Ingesting vigour and we shall see them rocking on the wire
As though it were autumn. They'll be gone away

All those handfuls of heart, nerve, appetite, over more
Unnourishing water to some lucky thatch or sweet
Dust and darkness of a barn and a family of humans
Whose year, emptying of hope, would sadden badly

If they didn't arrive. Our rock here is a landfall.
On the still nervous air the need and the grace of swallows
Continue imaginable for an hour or so. Love?
Nothing in a swallow says, I don't want to leave this place.

David Constantine

CAMOMILE TEA

Outside the sky is light with stars;
There's a hollow roaring from the sea.
And, alas! for the little almond flowers,
The wind is shaking the almond tree.

How little I thought, a year ago,
in the horrible cottage upon the Lee
That he and I should be sitting so
And sipping a cup of camomile tea.

Light as feathers the witches fly,
The horn of the moon is plain to see;
By a firefly under a jonquil flower
A goblin toasts a bumble-bee.

We might be fifty, we might be five,
So snug, so compact, so wise are we!
Under the kitchen-table leg
My knee is pressing against his knee.

Our shutters are shut, the fire is low,
The tap is dripping peacefully;
The saucepan shadows on the wall
Are black and round and plain to see.

Katherine Mansfield

SONNET 18

Shall I compare thee to a Summer's day?
Thou art more lovely and more temperate.
Rough winds do shake the darling buds of May,
And summer's lease hath all too short a date.
Sometime too hot the eye of heaven shines,
And often is his gold complexion dimmed;
And every fair from fair sometimes declines,
By chance, or nature's changing course, untrimmed:
But thy eternal summer shall not fade
Nor lose possession of that fair thou ow'st,
Nor shall Death brag thou wand'rest in his shade
When in eternal lines to time thou grow'st
So long as men can breathe or eyes can see,
So long live this, and this gives life to thee.

William Shakespeare

DESIRE

Did we feel desire? We felt it. We felt desire.
And what did we do with it? We suffered it
Behind the ribs, between the eyes and the ears,
In bowel and groin, as if struggling for breath,
As if we had been tackled or felled or had fallen
Out of a normal day onto a fist.
Our own palms sweated and prickled,
We peered out between our fingers. It had not seen us.

What did we do next? We read it, we got it by heart;
We put our ears to it and heard its little lungs
Huffing. We kept it warm, we fed it sweet things,
We sang to it, we turned it on its bed,
Plumped its pillow, cleared away the pans.
We held it close, it smelled yeasty, it smelled of soil.
What did we do? For a year we harboured it,
As if we were a modest town by a bay

And it dropped anchor, furled its sails, ran up its pennants...
The beautiful sailors with their sharp starched blue flaps,
The captain a wingless angel... no, the captain a man,
And at night the Chinese lanterns, bobbing, enchanting,
An ensemble of pipes, tabors and a fiddle
Shuffling the heart, making it dance. It danced.
We watched from the quay and never went aboard.
They urged and urged us but we never went aboard.

One day it was all over. We woke, it had gone.
Like when the circus leaves a suburb lifeless,
Or it's Epiphany and all the lighted trees
Smoulder in back yards and the smoke makes tears.

We turned to one another then with nothing to hold
But one another. We stayed in the town by the bay.
A moon swelled out of the sea and, once risen, abated
Into the now literal night we inhabit together.

Michael Schmidt

IT'S ALL I HAVE TO BRING TODAY

It's all I have to bring today,
This, and my heart beside,
This, and my heart, and all the fields,
And all the meadows wide.
Be sure you count, should I forget,
Someone the sum could tell,
This, and my heart, and all the bees
Which in the clover dwell.

Emily Dickinson

NO

No one is ever good enough,
or kind enough.
No one stays awake
through the lovely rush of rain which fills our dark.
No one can hold the music.
They are counting coins or frowning
They are toppling, they are drowning.
No one is good.

But nothing is as quick as us,
no screen can match us
tape's whirr catch us
nothing tilts like sun
to light from sad.
Nothing in all history
can reach to take your hand from me,
The dark, the rain's gift, O
we should be glad.

Alison Brackenbury

SHE HAS LOST HER VOICE

and will not get it back: it wandered out
into the street and kept on walking
where she couldn't call it. It walked out
through cat-tails and breathing marshes
to the lake, its feet hardly denting the water,
not thinking of thirst or hunger,
or worrying who might follow.

It walked over the fields singing
with its name on a hand-written label
so it could reach its destination.
It walked away from the war
still raging in her thin body,
travelling barefoot and hatless
to a place that might still be peaceful.

It travelled through low sun
and leaf-storms and early morning,
over ruts and frozen grasses
that spiked its soles with burning.
No luggage, no rusting hand-cart
piled with pots, no moth-eaten blanket,
no furniture it had no use for.

It didn't care who heard
its farewell to fear or yearning.
It simply walked away
out of earshot, with its naked head
held high, as far as it was able.

Susan Wicks

AMAZON

It begins –
Maybe when she's dressing, her fingers tucked
under the wire of her bra.

Or idly in the bath,
their familiar weight
made light of,

or in the mirror, one arm ballerinaed high,
the other testing the water
of her own flesh.

A mote under the skin
settling in her breast,
soft but hard as cartilage, and busy with its own beginning.

*

He tells her kindly enough, and anyway
she knows what is coming, or rather what's already there,

by the way he offers the seat,
his practised look of concern and the slow pace of his voice

that keeps the end of what he has to say
always at arm's length.

She hears the words he uses
and is quietly surprised by how language can do this:

how a certain order can carry so much chaos,
and how that word, with its hard C of cruelty

and soft c of uncertainty,
seems so fitted to the task.

But then she has to leave the surgery
and walk into her new world, so startingly the same:

the dustbins flowering with rubbish,
shoes for sale at the side of the street and the buses

redding past as if nothing has happened.

*

November 5th and her first outing since,
pale in the Autumn air, the night behind her,
tic-tac sparks from the fire streaming away on the wind.

All of us masked in the flame's hot soul,
writing with sparklers,
our names trailing their furious heads.

Her youngest gives her a bottle of champagne,
one that he's saved for this,
her coming back to us.

It is single-serving size, his size.
She wrings its neck gently, easing it open
but allows him the final give,

the pop and smoky release of its cork,
which he keeps, holding it tight in his fist.
She watches his fingers work around it,

under his coat's pocket, as he feels its shape:
soft but hard, stubborn to the touch, just like the bump
in the middle of the night that started all this in the first place.

*

She's all the way back now,
her life fitting about her once more
like old clothes pulled on from the changing room floor.

But her mind is still faceted, cut from the brink
her body brought it to,
and with it, she dreams.

Sometimes of the weight of its going,
the invisible twin she rises to touch
only to find skin over bone.

Or sometimes of how it was before,
holding sun-curled photos of the past.
But mostly of a day in the future,

when she will choose the nudist night to visit the pool,
where she will walk slow and slim
all the way to the deep end and enter the water an Amazon,

able to draw her bow further and deeper than other women.

Owen Sheers

ARS POETICA
for A.J.

Every elegy a love-poem; every love-poem
a kind of elegy. You live between
closeness and loss, fear and reward,
and look up to both as if to parents –
they knew what you were even before
you knew it yourself.
                              Then seemed to relent,
on the secret logic of whim:

till you turn and see each again,
waiting it out in the summer garden, where trees
fan green plumage over gravelled walks,
implying – footsteps. Or they'll shift, like breezes,
round the open window where you talk
on your cell-phone to this month's lover:
See, they say. It goes on. It's never over.

Fiona Sampson

GOOD HEDGES

He wants the holly tree cut down to size,
the holly tree where the birds are sound, and safe
from his cat whose snickering impersonation
of birdsong – more like the din a mincer makes –
fools no-one, and charms nothing out of the trees.

He wants us to tidy up the pyracantha sprouting
its fire-thorns and berry-laden fractals, and clip
the brambles, the lilacs, everything wild.
Next he'll want the hedgehog's spikes filed down,
the moles claws bound up with green twine

– already he's replaced his own hair with ginger nylon.
His light he says is being blocked. It's dark
where he is. He has a point – so many deaths
in these few houses, it's like something
loosed from the bible. One lucky escape, though:

the bearded roofer, one along, who lost
his footing, high on the scaffolding, and fell,
with his deck of tiles, on his shoulder and skull.
Sometimes tears come to his eyes for no reason
he can think of, but now the sun's out he sits again

on the patio, plucking from his banjo
some Appalachian strand of evergreen bluegrass
then an Irish reel where his fingers scale
a glittering ladder like a waterfall
so even the songbirds hush in the holly tree.

Jamie McKendrick

WINTERBOURNE

You wake at dawn, the moon like snow.
The red-cold sandstone doorstep glows
And stamped into the cast-iron lanes
Are brown dead leaves with silver veins.

White fields lead down between white trees
To a bank of blown glass reeds
Where light-enthralling silence lies
In one broad pane of dusty ice.

And standing on the lucid floor
You find beneath a face like yours
Able to look from world to world
Now the estranging water's stalled.

They stare and mouth. You start to speak.
The river-lid begins to creak.

Jacob Polley

I RELY ON YOU

I rely on you
like a Skoda needs suspension
like the aged need a pension
like a tramoline needs tension
like a bungee jump needs apprehension
I rely on you
like a camera needs a shutter
like a gambler needs a flutter
like a golfer needs a putter
like a buttered scone involves some butter
I rely on you
like an acrobat needs ice cool nerve
like a haipin needs a drastic curve
like an HGV needs endless derv
like an outside left needs a body swerve
I rely on you
like a handyman needs pliers
like an auctioneer needs buyers
like a laundromat needs driers
like The Good Life needed Richard Briers
I rely on you
like a water vole needs water
like a brick outhouse needs mortar
like a lemming to the slaughter
Ryan's just Ryan without his daughter
I rely on you

Hovis Presley

138

40-LOVE

40	love
middle	aged
couple	playing
ten	nis
when	the
game	ends
and	they
go	home
the	net
will	still
be	be
tween	them

Roger McGough

A SUBALTERN'S LOVE SONG

Miss J. Hunter Dunn, Miss J. Hunter Dunn,
Furnish'd and burnish'd by Aldershot sun,
What strenuous singles we played after tea,
We in the tournament – you against me!

Love-thirty, love-forty, oh! weakness of joy,
The speed of a swallow, the grace of a boy,
With carefullest carelessness, gaily you won,
I am weak from your loveliness, Joan Hunter Dunn.

Miss Joan Hunter Dunn, Miss Joan Hunter Dunn,
How mad I am, sad I am, glad that you won,
The warm-handled racket is back in its press,
But my shock-headed victor, she loves me no less.

Her father's euonymus shines as we walk,
And swing past the summer-house, buried in talk,
And cool the verandah that welcomes us in
To the six o'clock news and a lime-juice and gin.

The scent of the conifers, sound of the bath,
The view from my bedroom of moss-dappled path,
As I struggle with double-end evening tie,
For we dance at the Golf Club, my victor and I.

On the floor of her bedroom lie blazer and shorts,
And the cream-coloured walls are be-trophied with sports,
And westering, questioning settles the sun,
On your low-leaded window, Miss Joan Hunter Dunn.

The Hillman is waiting, the light's in the hall,
The pictures of Egypt are bright on the wall,
My sweet, I am standing beside the oak stair
And there on the landing's the light on your hair.

By roads "not adopted", by woodlanded ways,
She drove to the club in the late summer haze,
Into nine o'clock Camberley, heavy with bells
And mushroomy, pine-woody, evergreen smells

Miss Joan Hunter Dunn, Miss Joan Hunter Dunn,
I can hear from the car park the dance has begun,
Oh! full Surrey twilight! importunate band!
Oh! strongly adorable tennis-girl's hand!

Around us are Rovers and Austins afar,
Above us the intimate roof of the car,
And here on my right is the girl of my choice,
With the tilt of her nose and the charm of her voice.

And the scent of her wrap, and the words never said,
And the ominous, ominous dancing ahead.
We sat in the car park till twenty to one
And now I'm engaged to Miss Joan Hunter Dunn.

John Betjeman

INESSENTIAL THINGS

What do cats remember of days?

They remember the ways in from the cold,
The warmest spot, the place for food.
They remember the places of pain, their enemies,
The irritation of birds, the warm fumes of the soil,
The usefulness of dust.
They remember the creak of a bed, the sound
Of their owner's footsteps,
The taste of fish, the loveliness of cream.
Cats remember what is essential of days.
Letting all other memories go as if of no worth
They sleep sounder than we,
Whose hearts break remembering
So many inessential things.

Brian Patten

I PERCEIVED THE OUTLINE OF YOUR BREASTS

I perceived the outline of your breasts
through your Hallowe'en costume
I knew you were falling in love with me
because no other man could perceive
the advance of your bosom into his imagination
It was a rupture of your usual modesty
for me and me alone
through which you impressed upon my shapeless hunger
the incomparable and final outline of your breasts
like two deep fossil shells
which remained all night long and probably forever.

Leonard Cohen

THE CATCHER'S TAP

The old man slept shaded on the bank of the river and dreamed of a time when he was young. In the afternoon he always slept because the sun was too hot, and the reflected light upon the water hurt his eyes. On the path, not far from the old man, walked a small boy with a butterfly cupped in the palm of his hand. As he glanced down from behind a thicket of golden curls, the small boy noticed that the old man had left the door to his soul ajar. Almost at once the small boy released the butterfly, tapped lightly upon the door to the old man's soul, and crept in.

After an hour or two the old man stirred, rubbed his eyes with the backs of his hands, and woke from his sleep with a weight of sorrow in his soul. Despite his years the old man did not feel old, yet his dream had troubled him, and as he caught his reflection in the water he felt tears run down his face. 'I wish I had never been young,' he cried, as he brushed his wet cheeks, 'I could easily have borne being old if I had never been young, and my dreams tease me in the cruellest way. I am old, it is true,' wept the old man, 'and I have no heart for dreaming.'

He reclaimed his fallen hat from the dust of the river bank and watched as a butterfly opened and closed its wings on the felted head of a bulrush. 'I shall not come here to fish again,' said the old man as he carefully replaced the hat upon a dishevelled shock of silver hair; 'I have caught a fish which I can not throw back, and I am haunted by its sorrow,' he sighed, as he closed the door to his soul.

The old man left the river bank much earlier than usual and walked slowly home through the forest, stopping every so often to listen to the song of a bird, or to look up at the trees.

When he arrived at his cedar-boughed shack he was tired again, but was afraid to sleep. He stretched his frail and ancient frame over an old mattress and stared at the log wall above him. 'A wise man does not look for what he knows he can not find' he sighed, as he slowly closed his eyes.
The day was not yet over, and the old man knew that he would be asleep by nightfall. But, as he closed his eyes, he vowed that when he returned to the forest he would try to forget that he had been there before.
On the distant river bank bulrushes whispered mysterious, unheard in evening breezes; and somewhere deep in the old man's soul, a small boy searched for butterflies.

Chris Tutton

SHE IS...

She is...
the Yin to my Yang
the I to my Ching
the See to my Saw
the Head to my Tails
the Lily of my Valley

Sir Paul McCartney

WHEN YOU ARE OLD

When you are old and grey and full of sleep,
And nodding by the fire, take down this book,
And slowly read, and dream of the soft look
Your eyes had once, and of their shadows deep;

How many loved your moments of glad grace,
And loved your beauty with love false or true,
But one man loved the pilgrim soul in you,
And loved the sorrows of your changing face;

And bending down beside the glowing bars,
Murmer, a little sadly, how Love fled
And paced upon the mountains overhead
And hid his face amid a crowd of stars.

W B Yeats

A SINGLE WEATHER
(Khazendar)

They've got gaps in them the best walls
– it was a geg the way we'd grip hands
then slip through that tall – tall
and tight – gap in the wall
yes we squinched through that fissure
came back again and again we did
under fruit that was fit to burst

I could hear you trapped in your own voice
as we made sleaked talk – worse and worse –
by a well that since we were kids
no one'd drawn a bucket from ever
– unlike the sky you were never the same
and come nightfall you were different again
you felt no right to go back – both it
and the will to return
you'd let them slip

Tom Paulin

DIAGNOSIS

Twenty-one hours of daylight
now it's close to mid-summer,
and although most birds know
when to rest, posting themselves

like furtive love-notes into gaps
between stones in the harbour wall,
seagulls decide to tough it out,
rolling through the small hours

at head-height, too exhausted
to flap their wings or even feed.
The lacklustre cries they give,
starting another slow journey

to Scapa Flow and back, mean
What do you want? Get some sleep.
My reply is to keep watching waves
slosh to and fro over the dead ships

as though they were the only things
to keep me awake here, which anyone
looking down from the granite hotel
and the road behind would also think,

since they cannot see you as I do, alive
in your illness and walking on the water,
but disappearing whenever the light shifts
and the sea beneath reveals itself again.

Andrew Motion

HANDS

We first recognised each other as if we were siblings,
and when we held hands your touch
made me stupidly happy.

Hold my hand, you said in the hospital.

You had big hands, strong hands, gentle
as those of a Mediterranean father
caressing the head of a child.

Hold my hand, you said. *I feel
I won't die while you are here.*

You took my hand on our first aeroplane
and in opera houses, or watching
a video you wanted me to share.

Hold my hand, you said. *I'll fall asleep
and won't even know you're not there.*

Elaine Feinstein

PRAISE SONG FOR MY MOTHER

You were
water to me
deep and bold and fathoming

You were
moon's eye to me
pull and grained and mantling

You were
sunrise to me
rise and warm and steaming

You were
the fishes red gill to me
the flame tree's spread to me
the crab's leg/the fried plantain smell
                    replenishing replenishing

Go to your wide futures, you said.

Grace Nichols

THE ROAD NOT TAKEN

Two roads diverged in a yellow wood,
And sorry I could not travel both
And be one traveller, long I stood
And looked down one as far as I could
To where it bent in the undergrowth;

Then took the other, as just as fair,
And having perhaps the better claim,
Because it was grassy and wanted wear;
Though as for that the passing there
Had worn them really about the same,

And both that morning equally lay
In leaves no step had trodden black.
Oh, I kept the first for another day!
Yet knowing how way leads on to way,
I doubted if I should ever come back.

I shall be telling this with a sigh
Somewhere ages and ages hence:
Two roads diverged in a wood, and I--
I took the one less travelled by,
And that has made all the difference.

Robert Frost

FOR WHOM THE BELL TOLLS

No man is an island,
Entire of itself.
Each is a piece of the continent,
A part of the main.
If a clod be washed away by the sea,
Europe is the less.
As well as if a promontory were.
As well as if a manner of thine own
Or of thine friend's were.
Each man's death diminishes me,
For I am involved in mankind.
Therefore, send not to know
For whom the bell tolls,
It tolls for thee.

John Donne

SUMMER

Is a lazy god, and all promises.
He says he will never leave,
Was a long time coming
With swallows in his air –
Petulant, weeping.
Waking early one morning
I watch him from the bedroom window
Barefoot on the wet grass,
Stalking the garden and beside himself
With all the brilliant flowers.
With soft, dry hands he soothes their heavy heads.
My children's books, too,
That were carelessly left on the lawn all night,
Unread and ruined by the rain.

Deryn Rees-Jones

THE ARRIVALS

I pull the bed slowly open, I
open the lips of the bed, get
the stack of fresh underpants
out of the suitcase -- peach, white,
cherry, quince, pussy willow, I
choose a colour and put them on,
I travel with the stack for the stack's caress,
dry and soft. I enter the soft
birth-lips of the bed, take off my
glasses, and the cabbage-roses on the curtain
blur to Keats's peonies, the
ochre willow holds a cloud
the way a skeleton holds flesh
and it passes, does not hold it.
The bed fits me like a walnut shell its
meat, my hands touch the upper corners,
The lower, my feet. It is so silent
I hear the choirs of wild silence, the
maenads of the atoms. Is this what it feels like
to have a mother? The sheets are heavy
cream, whipped. Ah, here is my mother,
or rather here she is not, so this is
paradise. But surely that
was paradise, when her Jell-O nipple was the
size of my own fist, in front of my
face--out of its humped runkles those
several springs of milk, so fierce
almost fearsome. What did I think
in that brain gridded for thought, its cups
loaded with languageless rennet? And at night,
when they timed me, four hours of screaming, not a

minute more, four, those quatrains of
icy yell, then the cold tap water
to get me over my shameless hunger,
what was it like to be there when that
hunger was driven into my structure at such
heat it alloyed that iron? Where have I
been while this person is leading my life
with her patience, will and order? In the garden;
on the bee and under the bee; in the
crown gathering cumulus and
flensing it from the boughs, weeping a
rehearsal for the rotting and casting off of our
flesh, the year we slowly throw it
off like clothing by the bed covers of our lover, and dive
                                                    under.

Sharon Olds

PICTURE THIS

You come into focus most clearly on windy Mondays,
Grandad's shirt sleeves applauding on the line,
curtains boiling at windows. Your cheeks, normally pale,
slapped red by sudden gusts; I see you bending,
stiff-backed, to retrieve a peg or yank a dandelion,
then your apron snarls itself up and your dress
lifts sharply to reveal the tops of stockings pinching
mottled thighs. I can hold you there for several seconds
until your hair escapes its pins and leaves you blurred.

Catherine Smith

"World is suddener than we fancy it"
Louis MacNeice

World is very all at once;
breaks apart the night with grinding gears,
flares orange neon, sulphurous, against closed lids,
then crashes in through windows green with birdsong.
Trapped in a box it blasts out barking
"Last night another soldier...A crippled plane..."
A slow drip drip of black ice melting,
apocalypse seeping through the cochlea's labyrinth.

World is more demanding,
stands fretful at the bedroom door at 3a.m.
relentless, reproducing in a Petri dish,
the cosmos on a microscope's slide,
dancing in the cilia of protozoa
suspended in a drop of water.

World is unsentimental;
in the kiss of a praying mantis,
the black widow's embrace.
It constantly surprises – the sudden inflation
of a red bladder in a green lizard's neck,
the sudden infatuation with a waiter at Pizza Express.
The sudden explosion of cells in an erstwhile biddable breast.

It's arbitrary, wilful, changes the rules mid-game
which ends before you're ready.

Marion Hobday

NO ADHESIVE NECESSARY

Past the Hide 'n Seek lingerie range, beyond Naughty
Nurse and Hail Mary sets, to a screened-off area with
rows of jelly-coloured vibrators and Jiggle Balls. By the
time I'm examining a five foot inflatable penis, she's
close. *Need any help?* That confidential smile. *Yes, do
you have nipples?* She's not sure, she'll check. *I've lost
mine,* I add, for authenticity.

At home, I press the salmon-coloured discs back to
back – a minature UFO – then peel them apart, lick
their flat sides, choosing where to place my *one size*
nipples: near or far, high or low. They sit over the stripes
of white scar like elastoplast. Under a T shirt they
appear home-grown, virtually real. When I touch them
they're always firm.

Clare Best

THE ROSE IN THE DEEPS OF HIS HEART

All things uncomely and broken,
all things worn-out and old,
The cry of a child by the roadway,
the creak of a lumbering cart,

The heavy steps of the ploughman,
splashing the wintry mould,
Are wronging your image that blossoms
A rose in the deeps of my heart.

The wrong of unshapely things
is a wrong too great to be told;
I hunger to build them anew
and sit on a green knoll apart,

With the earth and the sky and the water,
remade, like a casket of gold
For my dreams of your image that blossoms
a rose in the deeps of my heart.

W B Yeats

RENUNCIATION

from the irish of Séathrún Céitinn

Dear woman, with your wiles,
You'd best remove your hand,
Though you burn with love's fire,
I'm no more an active man.

Look at the grey on my head,
See how my body droops,
Think of my sluggish blood --
What would you have me do?

It's not desire I lack.
Don't bend low like that again.
Love can live without the act
Forever, slender minx.

Withdraw your lips from mine,
Strong as the inclination is,
Don't brush against my skin,
It could lead to wantonness.

The intricacy of curls,
Soft eyes clear as dew,
The pale sight of your curves,
Give pleasure to me now.

Bar what the body craves,
And lying with you requires,
I'll do for our love's sake,
Dear woman, with your wiles.

Maurice Riordan

CELIA, CELIA

When I am sad and weary,
When I think all hope has gone,
When I walk along High Holborn
I think of you with nothing on.

Adrian Mitchell

AUDIT

March days we plan
with lists, yet life
keeps happening.

Mornings, I hide from light
as you leave, your bag fat
with textbooks.

March brings me low –
days of sleety snow
and waiting for another
mapping of the body
in this month of its
annual audit.

Usually, I'm like a wilful
child with a toy trumpet
blasting my way through
but March silences me.

These nights I dream
I'm in a famine field
weakly negotiating
the potato ridges,
my head unhinged
from a cabbage only
diet.

When you're gone
I walk the mornings
Then stare the afternoons
away at the big screen.

162

At dinner we talk
other people or politics.
We practise normality,
our gauge set taut.

In sleep you mutter
things I can't decipher
and hold me so fast
I wake.

Today I'll be in a hospital
paper gown again,
but when I daydream
we trampoline together.

Clairr O'Connor

THERE IS ANOTHER SKY

There is another sky,
Ever serene and fair,
And there is another sunshine,
Though it be darkness there;
Never mind faded forests, Austin,
Never mind silent fields -
Here is a little forest,
Whose leaf is ever green;
Here is a brighter garden,
Where not a frost has been;
In its unfading flowers
I hear the bright bee hum:
Prithee, my brother,
Into my garden come!

Emily Dickinson

A DREAM

In visions of the dark night
I have dreamed of joy departed –
But a waking dream of life and light
Hath left me broken-hearted.

Ah! What is not a dream by day
To him whose eyes are cast
On things around him with a ray
Turned back upon the past?

That holy dream – that holy dream,
While all the world were chiding,
Hath cheered me as a lovely beam
A lonely spirit guiding.

What though that light, thro' storm and night,
So trembled from afar –
What could there be more purely bright
In Truth's day star?

Edgar Allan Poe

THE PASSIONATE SHEPHERD TO HIS LOVE

Come live with me and be my love,
And we will all the pleasures prove
That hills and valleys, dales and fields,
Or woods or sleepy mountain yields.

And we will sit upon the rocks,
And see the shepherds feed their flocks
By shallow rivers, to whose falls
Melodious birds sing madrigals.

And I will make thee beds of roses
And a thousand fragrant posies;
A cap of flowers and a kirtle
Embroider'd all with leaves of myrtle.

A gown made of the finest wool
Which from our pretty lambs we pull;
Fair-lined slippers for the cold,
With buckles of the purest gold.

A belt of straw and ivy-buds
With coral clasps and amber studs;
And if these pleasures may thee move,
Come live with me and be my love.

The shepherd swains shall dance and sing
For thy delight each May morning:
If these delights thy mind may move,
Then live with me and be my love.

Christopher Marlowe

THE TRANSPOSITION
OF DESIRE

I miss the play of your light
upon my shadow and stone
where I dream undiscovered
apostrophes.
I miss your tender hedgerows
gathering lustrous threads of
morning silk you
braided for drawstrings of
our twilight's skyline.

Chris Tutton

LOVE CUTS

Love cuts
love juts out
and you walk right into it.

Love cuts
love comes and goes
love's a rose
first you smell the flower
then the thorn goes up your nostril
love gives you chocolates
then love gives you the chop
It doesn't like to linger.

Love cuts
love shuts up shop
and shuts it on your finger
love cuts
what isn't very nice is
love leaves you in slices.

Love cuts
love's very sharp
a harpoon through an easy chair
a comb of honey in your hair
just wait until the bees come home
and find you just relaxing there.

Love cuts
love's claws
evacuate that heart of yours

and leave it on the sleeve it wipes
its nose on.

Love cuts, love guts the fish
of what you wish for
and leaves it in the airing cupboard.

Love cuts
love huts fall down
as all the walls get falser.

Love cuts
love struts around on stilts of balsa wood
love cuts love gives you a sweeping bow
then ploughs a furrow deep above your eyebrow
love cuts
love curtseys
then nuts you
where it really hurtseys.

John Hegley

ATLAS

There is a kind of love called maintenance
Which stores the WD40 and knows when to use it

Which checks the insurance, and doesn't forget
The milkman; which remembers to plant bulbs;

Which answers letters; which knows the way
The money goes; which deals with dentists

And Road Fund Tax and meeting trains,
And postcards to the lonely; which upholds

The permanently rickety elaborate
Structures of living, which is Atlas.

And maintenance is the sensible side of love,
Which knows what time and weather are doing
To my brickwork; insulates my faulty wiring;
Laughs at my dry rotten jokes; remembers
My need for gloss and grouting; which keeps
My suspect edifice upright in air;
As Atlas did the sky.

U A Fanthorpe

THE MARRIAGE

They will fit, she thinks,
but only if her backbone
cuts exactly into his rib cage,
and only if his knees
dock exactly under her knees
and all four
agree on a common angle.

All would be well
if only
they could face each other.

Even as it is
there are compensations
for having to meet
nose to neck
chest to scapula
groin to rump
when they sleep.

They look, at least,
as if they were going
in the same direction.

Anne Stevenson

ON THE SAILING BOAT
a painting by Caspar David Friedrich

So on the prow the lovers lean,
She in red velvet, he in green,
Their hands clasped, hot and keen.

Their eyes stare into painted sun.
Who guides the sheltering sail? No one.
Their trip has just begun.

I would rush in, knot the line firm,
To hold them in the glittering storm,
Wrap narrow shoulders warm.

Oh, if you make it, you must land,
Find bills, lost jobs, misunderstand
A child hot in your hand,

And then another. Will you fail?
But look, the sea sleeps, still and pale.
First teach them how to sail.

Alison Brackenbury

HOW WE CRY

My mother cries hard tears, tight
and slicing her face like steel.

My sister's tears are packed away, her eyes
balloons filled with water, their glassy skins
aching with weight.

I saw my father cry once – perched on the edge
of the tweed covered sofa in the living-room,
his father's death dragging
his face to his knees.

                            These days when I cry
I think of rain, how the sky falls down and blankets the hills,
flattens rivers to a torrent of mud; and how
a heron can still rise through it – away from the bruised
                                                  banks,
a grey raggedy flight upstream.

Lynne Rees

I 'D LIKE TO LIVE IN A FRENCH FILM

where the thin tea-brown light
paints me wise and beautiful
and the sound of my neighbour
playing Elgar on his violin
seeps through the walls
and makes
a stinging soundtrack
to my life.
Nothing will be bland:
you will be addicted
to my skin,
you will smoke
stumpy Gauloise cigarettes,
fill your car
with lust and violet clouds
as you drive through storms
dodging
monstrous wind-fall trees
and crashed telegraph poles
just to get to me,
just to plant little kisses
like forget-me-nots
at the top of my thighs.
And in the morning,
every morning
the wet streets will shine
like pewter,
the world will sound
like Paris and rain.

The air will smell
of hot sugar,
swollen dough
and carousels.

Gaia Holmes

YOU LEFT ME

You left me, sweet, two legacies, –
    A legacy of love
A Heavenly Father would content,
    Had he the offer of;

You left me boundaries of pain
    Capacious as the sea,
Between eternity and time,
    Your consciousness and me.

Emily Dickinson

HAPPINESS

This perfect love can find no words to say.
What words are left, still sacred for our use,
That have not suffered the sad world's abuse,
And figure forth a gladness dimmed and gray?
Let us be silent still, since words convey
But shadowed images, wherein we lose
The fulness of love's light; our lips refuse
The fluent commonplace of yesterday.

Then shall we hear beneath the brooding wing
Of silence what abiding voices sleep,
The primal notes of nature, that outring
Man's little noises, warble he or weep,
The song of the morning stars together sing,
The sound of deep that calleth unto deep.

Edith Wharton

LOVE'S PHILOSOPHY

The fountains mingle with the river,
And the rivers with the ocean;
The winds of Heaven mix for ever,
With a sweet emotion;
Nothing in the world is single,
All things by a law divine
In one another's being mingle –
Why not I with thine?

See the mountains kiss high Heaven
And the waves clasp one another;
No sister-flower would be forgiven
If it disdained its brother;
And the sunlight clasps the earth,
And the moonbeams kiss the sea –
What are all those kissings worth
If thou kiss not me?

Percy Bysshe Shelley

MRS LOGAN

In my final term at Junior School I enjoyed the most entertaining and instructive lesson in all of my schooldays, inspired by Mrs Logan who took PE in the school hall on the first floor. For some reason we boys were required to remove our shorts, with their stains and comforting marbles, in order to do the excercises in our underpants. By the age of eleven this had become extremely embarrassing. We felt sheepish and vulnerable in front of the girls, who had no such humiliating requirement. As we gingerly stripped off one day Tom Simpson got his shorts caught on the end of his foot and kicked them free with such alacrity that they sailed through the air, straight out of an open window and down to the playground below.

There was a moment while everyone took in this stupendous occurence. Then, of course, came shrieks of laughter. Tom Simpson, stricken with shame, began to cry as all the embarrassment we other boys felt suddenly rushed from us to him. The girls were laughing hard too. Everyone, except Mrs Logan and Simpson, was screaming in hilarity. Poor old Tom. Eventually Mrs Logan regained an uneasy silence but not control. The lesson was in disarray until, in a moment of inspiration she surely never surpassed in her teaching career, Mrs Logan shouted. "RIGHT! ALL YOU BOYS, THROW YOUR SHORTS OUT THE WINDOW!"

What a fantastic invitation! Tom's emasculation was forgotten; he stopped sobbing as we queued up to launch our shorts through the window. The occasion had become funny in a good way such that even Mrs Logan and Tom were enjoying themselves. In fact Tom now looked like a trailblazing hero. The children in the class below must also surely have relished the strange sight of the sky raining boys' shorts. As we trouped down, to retrieve them, chortling and tittering, our new-found solidarity meant that the giggling girls now seemed admiring rather than threatening and I learnt the truth that one man in public in his pants is pitiable but ten is a possee of fun.

I wonder if anyone else who was there that day remembers this incident? Tom Simpson may and possibly Mrs Logan too if she is still alive, but I doubt anyone else does. The images of youth that stay with us into adulthood often seem to others arbitrary and without apparent significance. Or maybe it was for the others in the class the astounding event that lives in my mind. At any rate, ever since that PE lesson the phrase has periodically returned to me, acting as a call to arms, a bold plan in a tricky situation, an invitation to creative mayhem.

Boys throw your shorts out the window.

Arthur Smith

WIND AND WINDOW FLOWER

Lovers, forget your love,
And listen to the love of these,
She a window flower,
And he a winter breeze.

When the frosty window veil
Was melted down at noon,
And the caged yellow bird
Hung over her in tune,

He marked her through the pane,
He could not help but mark,
And only passed her by
To come again at dark.

He was a winter wind,
Concerned with ice and snow,
Dead weeds and unmated birds,
And little of love could know.

But he sighed upon the sill,
He gave the sash a shake,
As witness all within
Who lay that night awake.

Perchance he half prevailed
To win her for the flight
From the firelit looking glass
And warm stove-window light.

But the flower leaned aside
And thought of naught to say,
And morning found the breeze
A hundred miles away.

Robert Frost

A CELTIC BLESSING

May the road rise up to meet you.
May the wind be always at your back.
May the sun shine warm upon your face;
the rains fall soft upon your fields and until we meet
again, may God hold you in the palm of His hand.

Traditional

ENDYMION
(Extract)

A thing of beauty is a joy for ever;
Its loveliness increases; it will never
Pass into nothingness; but still will keep
A bower quiet for us, and a sleep
Full of sweet dreams, and health, and quiet breathing.
Therefore, on every morrow, are we wreathing
A flowery band to bind us to the earth,
Spite of despondence, of the inhuman dearth
Of noble natures, of the gloomy days,
Of all the unhealthy and o'er-darkn'd ways
Made for our searching: yes, in spite of all,
Some shape of beauty moves away the pall
From our dark spirits, such the sun, the moon,
Trees old and young, sprouting a shady boon
For simple sheep; and such are daffodils
With the green world they live in; and clear rills
That for themselves a cooling covert make
'Gainst the hot season; the mid-forest brake,
Rich with a sprinkling of fair musk-rose blooms:
And such too is the grandeur of the dooms
We have imagined for the mighty dead;
All lovely tales that we have heard or read:
An endless fountain of immortal drink,
Pouring unto us from the heaven's brink.

John Keats

ALL THAT IS GOLD DOES NOT GLITTER

All that is gold does not glitter,
Not all those who wander are lost;
The old that is strong does not wither,
Deep roots are not reached by the frost.
From the ashes a fire shall be woken,
A light from the shadows shall spring;
Renewed shall be blade that was broken,
The crownless again shall be king.

J R R Tolkein

INCANTATA
(Excerpt)
In memory of Mary Farl Powers

Of the day your father came to call, of your leaving your sick-
room
in what can only have been a state of delirium,
of how you simply wouldn't relent
from your vision of a blind
watch-maker, of your fatal belief that fate
governs everything from the honey-rust of your father's
terrier's
eyebrows to the horse that rusts and rears
in the furrow, of the furrows from which we can no more
deviate

than they can from themselves, no more than the map of
Europe
can be redrawn, than that Hermes might make a harp from his
harpe,
than that we must live in a vale
of tears on the banks of the Lagan or the Foyle,
Than that what we have is a done deal,
than that the Irish Hermes,
Lugh, might have leafed through his vast herbarium
for the leaf that had it within it, Mary, to annoint and anneal,

than that Lugh of the Long Arm might have found in the
                                        midst of *lus*
na leac or *lus na treatha* or *Framc-lus,*
in the midst of eyebright, or speedwell, or tansy, an antidote,
than that this *Incantata*
might have you look up from your plate of copper or zinc
on which you've etched the row upon row
of army-worms, than that you might reach out, arrah,
and take in your ink-stained hands my own hands stained
                                        with ink.

Paul Muldoon

NOVA
from **A Garland For Linda**

Are You there?
God where are You?

Are you hiding in Your Heaven?
Or beneath Your deepest sea?
Was there something in our past imperfect?
Or is it something that we should have known?

Are You there?
God where are You?

Are you hiding, God?
Are You hiding in the rain?
Are you hiding?

I am here

I am in every song you sing
In the wings of a rising lark
Through the darkness to the morning light.
I am present in everything.

I am here as first a new-born babe
Opens eyes on the universe.

I am here
I am here now
I am with you

I am here as every flake of snow
Washes white on the countryside.
As each green blade stretches for the sun.
I am here watching over them.

I am here as first a new-born babe
Opens eyes on the universe.
With each step I'll be that arm that guides
Now and then till the end of time.

Amen.

Sir Paul McCartney

A heart that loves is always young

Greek Proverb

ACKNOWLEDGEMENTS

'Counting' by Fleur Adcock from "Poems 1960-2000" (Bloodaxe Books 2000) 'If' from "Transformatrix" by Patience Agbabi, first published in Great Britain by Canongate Books Ltd., 14 High Street, Edinburgh EH1 1TE. 'Carrying My Wife' by Moniza Alvi from "Splitworld Poems 1990-2005" (Bloodaxe Books 2005) 'Provisions' by Margaret Atwood ©OWTOAD Reproduced with permission of Curtis Brown Group.

'Old Love' by Francesca Beard is from her Chapbook, "Cheap"(www. francescabeard.com).'No Adhesive Necessary' by Clare Best, published in Smiths Knoll (2009) ©'The Subaltern's Love Song' by John Betjeman. Reproduced by permission of John Murray (publishers). 'No' by Alison Brackenbury published in the Times Literary Supplement.

Debjani Chatterjee's 'Interludes' was commissioned for the Poems in the Waiting Room Project by David Hart and Rogan Woolf in 2000 and published in her collection "Namsakar. New and Selected Poems" (Redbeck Press 2004) 'Cutting the Population' by Marvin Cheeseman first published in "Full Metal Jacket Potato" The Bad Press. 'I Almost Went to Bed' and 'Beneath My Hands' from "The Spice-Box of Earth" by Leonard Cohen, published by Jonathan Cape. Reprinted by permission of the Random House Group. 'I Perceived the Outline of Your Breasts' from "The Energy of Slaves" by Leonard Cohen, published by Jonathan Cape. Reprinted by permission of the Random House Group. 'I Wanna Be Yours' by John Cooper Clarke reproduced with kind permission of Phil Jones and with thanks to John Cooper Clarke. 'The Health Scare' by Wendy Cope appears with the author's permission.

'Too Heavy' by Julia Darling from "Sudden Collapses in Public Places", is reprinted by kind permission of Julia Darling's family and of Arc Publications.'The Present' by Michael Donaghy from "Dances Learned Last Night" Published by Picador ©Michael Donaghy 2000. Reproduced by permission of Picador and Maddy Paxman. 'A Day by the Sea and